THE 12 LAWS OF SUCCESS

(Previously published as THE SECRET REVEALED)

Charles Prosper

Third Edition February 2015

Global Publishing Company • Los Angeles, California

THE 12 LAWS OF SUCCESS

(Previously published as THE SECRET REVEALED in 2007 & 2011)

by Charles Prosper

Copyright © 2015 by Charles Prosper
All Rights Reserved

First Printing   September 2007
Second Printing   August 2011
Third Printing   February 2015

NO PART OF THIS BOOK MAY BE REPRODUCED, IN WHOLE OR IN PART, IN ANY FORM BY ANY MEANS, DIGITAL, ELECTRONIC OR MECHANICAL, INCLUDING PHOTOCOPY SYSTEMS, WITHOUT PERMISSION IN WRITING FROM THE AUTHOR, ADDRESS INQUIRIES TO GLOBAL PUBLISHING COMPANY, 2658 GRIFFITH PARK BLVD. SUITE 349, LOS ANGELES, CA 90039.

Book layout design and cover design by Charles Prosper

LIBRARY OF CONGRESS CATALOG CARD DATA

ISBN–13 978-0-943845-63-0

PRINTED IN THE UNITED STATES OF AMERICA

14 13 12 11 10 9 8 7 6 5 4 3

**In memory of my brother, Bernard.
(1952 - 2011)**

CONTENTS

Introduction. xi

Part 1 — THE 12 GREAT LAWS OF SUCCESS 1

Chapter 1. THE 12 GREAT LAWS OF THE UNIVERSE 3
    The Twilight Zone Episode "A Nice Place to Visit" 3
    God Became So Bored That He Became You. 6
    Law #1   The Law of Goal Setting. 6
    Law #2   The Law of Belief. 6
    Law #3   The Law of Positive Expectation. 6
    Law #4   The Law of Detachment. 6
    Law #5   The Law of Attraction.. 7
    Law #6   The Law of Planning. 7
    Law #7   The Law of Willingness to Do Whatever It Takes . . 7
    Law #8   The Law of Immediate Action. 7
    Law #9   The Law of Persistence. 7
    Law #10 The Law of Money. 7
    Law #11 The Law of Gratitude 7
    Law #12 The Law of Giving. 7

Chapter 2. THE LAW OF GOAL SETTING 9
    Why You <u>Must</u> Have Goals 9
    How to Discover Your Life Purpose 11
    Purpose vs. Goals 12
    Goals Are the Many Paths of Your Life Purpose 12
    The Transformational Power of a Goal 13
    The Processional Effect. 13
    Choosing A Worthwhile Goal 14
    Discovering Your Purpose Through Serving Others. 14
    Why Do You Exist? 14
    There Are No Accidents 15
    Everything Has a Purpose 15
    We Need You. 16
    You Are Unique (An Endangered Species) 16
    Giving: The Reason of All Life Purpose 16
    Stewards and Not Owners 17
    Everything Is On Loan. 17
    The 7-Step Goal Setting Success Formula 18
    Step # 1 Write Down Your Goal. 18
    Step # 2 Write Down When You Expect to Obtain the Goal. . 19
    Step # 3 Write Down Obstacles in the Way of Your Goal. . . 20
    Step # 4 Write Down the Needed People and Organizations. . 20
    Step # 5 Write Down A Plan of Action 23

Count to 20 for Plenty. 23
Step # 6 Write Down What You Need to Know or Learn. . . 26
Step # 7 Write Down *Why* This Goal is Important to You . . 26
What is the Meaning of Life? 27

Chapter 3. THE LAW OF BELIEF . . . . **.29**

What Exactly is a Belief? 29
Faith and Belief Are Synonymous 29
Thoughts Are Things. 30
What the Sages Have to Say About the Power of Belief. . . . 30
What You Say is What You Get 31

Chapter 4. THE LAW OF POSITIVE EXPECTATION . . . . **.33**

The Placebo Effect 34
What You Expect, You Get. 34
You Can Develop Your Positive Expectation Muscle 34

Chapter 5. THE LAW OF DETACHMENT . . . . **.37**

The Magic of Present Moment Living 37
Let Us Live Life Now (An Inspired Essay) by Charles Prosper. 38
What Does Detachment Mean? 41
Detachment is Acceptance, and Acceptance is Peace.. 41
Detachment is the Key to Happiness and Success 42

Chapter 6. THE LAW OF ATTRACTION . . . . **.45**

Isaac Newton's Law of Physics 46
The Rich Get Richer, and the Poor Get Poorer. 46
Thoughts Attract Like Thoughts 47
Nipping Negative Thoughts in the Bud 47
Notice What Your Are Feeling, for This is What You Attract . 49
Love & Fear Are Two Major Opposing Forces 49

Chapter 7. THE LAW OF PLANNING . . . . **.51**

The Two Major Aspects of the Law of Planning 51
Don't Ask for Opinions (From Family and Friends) 52
Don't Tell People What You Are Going to Do 53
You Are the Pregnant Mother of Your Dream. 54
The 7 Secret Steps to Planning 54

Chapter 8. THE LAW OF WILLINGNESS TO DO WHATEVER IT TAKES. . . . . **.57**

Action Leads to More Action. 58
Action Creates New Feelings, & New Feelings Create Actions. 58
Your Willingness to Do Whatever It Takes Tiggers Intuition . 59
Inspiration Unused is Merely Entertainment. 60

What Happens When You Are Not Willing 60
Willingness Is A Ready-to-Go-When-Instructed Mentally . . 61

Chapter 9. THE LAW OF IMMEDIATE ACTION **63**

The Universe Rewards Action! 63
Procrastination is the Monster of Failure. 63
Anything Worth Doing Is Worth Doing Lousy. 64
The Myth of Tomorrow 64
Strike While the Iron is Hot 65
Learn By Doing 65
Know When to Plan & Pray and When to Move & Make It . 65
God Speaks Through Circumstances. 66

Chapter 10. THE LAW OF PERSISTENCE **69**

The Way We See the Problem <u>Is</u> the Problem. 69
The Creed of Calvin Coolidge (Persistence) 70
Persistence and Faith are Synonymous 70
Persistence is the Continuous Choice of Positive Action . . .71
Inspired Action vs. Frantic Action 71
How Many Frogs Were Left? (A Riddle) 71
Are You a Flea, a Grasshopper, or a Goal Achiever? 72

Chapter 11. THE LAWS OF MONEY **75**

The First Law of Money is the Law of Saving Money. 75
The Second Law of Money is the Law of Control of Money. .76
The "Rich" Pauper. 77
Americans Are Afraid to Save-We Equate Saving with Lack ..78
The Third Law of Money-Pay Yourself First (Automatically) ..79
Sleep-Well-At-Night 3 Months Emergency Savings 81
When Is It an Emergency to Use Your Cash Savings? 83
The Myth of Borrowing Your Savings-And Putting It Back . 84
Your Savings Reflect Self-Worth & "Money Comfort Zone" ..84
Long Term Retirement Automatic Savings Account 85
Compound Interest by Automatically Saving $100 Month. ..86
Investment Automatic Savings Account 87
Everyone Should Have Some Type of Part-Time Business . ..87
Multiple Streams of Income-The Parthenon of Security . . .88
The Fourth Law of Money-You Must <u>*Enjoy*</u> Money. 88
The Fifth Law of Money-You Must <u>*Give*</u> Money 89
The Sixth Law of Money-You Must <u>*Invest*</u> Money 89
The Seventh Law of Money-Be <u>*Grateful*</u> for Money 89

Chapter 12. THE LAW OF GRATITUDE **91**

The Gratitude Diary-Recording Your Blessings One by One. .91
Gratitude is Prayer 92
Gratitude is Magnetic 93

Gratitude Prospers You. 93
Once Every 30 Days, Re-Read All of Your Entries 93

Chapter 13. THE LAW OF GIVING 95

Sharing is Having More 95
The Secret of Attracting Good Luck Everyday of Your Life. . 96
The Mystery Jogger 96
To Whom Do You Give Your Time? 97
Can You Play with Me Daddy?. 98
Giving Creates Happiness 99
The Law of Tithing 99

Part 2 – PRACTICAL APPLICATIONS OF THE LAWS OF SUCCESS 101

Chapter 14. HOW TO OVERCOME PROCRASTINATION. 103

Procrastination is the Root of Failure. 103
"Success is Doing What You Say You Will Do" 104
How Much Do You <u>Want</u> to Overcome Procrastination?. . 106
Why Do We Procrastinate? 106
Procrastination of Perfectionism (Fear of Self-Criticism). . 106
The Procrastination of Overwhelm (Fear of Failure) . . . 107
The Procrastination of Disapproval (Fear of Rejection) . . 107
Shyness Sucks 108
The 12 Steps to Total "Procrastination-Busting" 108
<u>Step 1</u>: Set the Task and Move Fast! 109
<u>Step 2</u>: Be Willing to Suffer Initially 110
<u>Step 3</u>: Visualize Yourself Doing the Task Easily 110
<u>Step 4</u>: Create and Carry Around a Goal Card 111
<u>Step 5</u>: Write Down a To-Do List the Night Before 111
<u>Step 6</u>: Repeat "Do It Now!" 10 Times Before the Task . . 112
<u>Step 7</u>: Create a "Reward System" after Each Task Done . 112
<u>Step 8</u>: Refuse to Make Excuses 113
<u>Step 9</u>: Begin with a Detailed Written Plan 113
<u>Step 10</u>: Eat an Elephant 113
<u>Step 11</u>: Start with the Most Difficult Task First 113
<u>Step 12</u>: Make an Appointment with Yourself 113

Chapter 15. TECHNIQUES OF CREATIVE THINKING. 115

What is Genius? 115
Left Brain/Right Brain Thinking 115
Creative Thinking through Creative Visualization 116

Chapter 16. CREATIVE DREAMING 119

More Than "Just a Dream". 119
Why You Dream. 121
An Owner's Manual 121

Who Dreams? 121
The Electroencephalograph (The EEG) 122
Some Famous Dreams 123
How to Remember Your Dreams 124
Motivation is the Key to Dream Recall 125
Programming Yourself to Remember Your Dreams 125
Your Morning Dream Recall Ritual 126
How to Keep a Dream Journal 127
How to Record Your Dreams with Your Eyes Closed . . . 128
The Key Elements of a Dream Journal 129
Your Weekly Dream Review 131
Your Monthy Dream Review 132
Your Yearly Summary 133
How to Learn to Interpret Your Dreams 134
Dream Dictionaries 134
Create Your Own Dream Glossary 135
What's Going On In Your Life? 135
The *Picture* Language of Dreams 136
What is a Metaphor? 136
Meaning is Multi-Layered 138
Speak As Your Dream Symbol 138
The "That's-Not-Good-Enough" Reaction 138
Speak to Your Dream Symbols in Seated Visualization . . . 139
Some Aspect of You 139
Recurrent Dreams 139
Nightmares 140
Dreamlettes 140
Form a Dream Study Group 141
Creative Problem Solving 141
Ask Your Dreams for Help 141
Allow 21 Days for Your Answer to Come 143
Acting on Your Dream Guidance 143
Lucid Dreaming–Know You're Dreaming while Dreaming. 143
What is a Lucid Dream? 144
The Twilight Zone Episode "Shadow Play" 145
How to Induce Lucid Dreams at Will 145
Visualization-Affirmation of Lucid Dream Induction . . . 146
The Pre-Bed Phase 146
The Middle-of-the-Night Phase 147
Overcoming Initial and Natural Resistance to Get Up . . . 148
Step-by-Step Procedure Phase II Lucid Dream Induction . 148
How to Control a Lucid Dream 150
The Pre-Lucid Phase of Lucid Dream Control 150
Stabilizing Your Lucid Dream Experience 150
False Awakenings 150
The Awesome Possibilities of Lucid Dreams 151

Chapter 17. FINAL THOUGHTS: WHO ARE YOU? **153**

The Divine Syllogism 153

INTRODUCTION

If you have not already figured it out, this book is an answer to the phenomenal bestselling "The Secret" by Rhonda Byrne. If you have not already heard about it or if you have not already read it, I highly recommend it as must-reading. You can easily find it at any major bookstore or you may obtain it online through Amazon.com. This book is amazing and the DVD version of "The Secret" is breathtaking. I love what Ms. Byrne did to introduce the world to the verities and truths of life that have been taught and expounded by sages, scholars and saints for centuries. What makes the book "The Secret" so good is its simplicity; attention is in every artistic detail of the book, from cover layout to internal page design. It's just beautiful!

"It's not important that you know everything–just the important things."–Miguel de Unamuno

What is emphasized in "The Secret" is the Law of Attraction. This is the law which states, "You become what you think about." "As a man thinketh in his heart, so is he." This law states that according to your predominant thought or thoughts about something, you attract to you all of the people, conditions, experiences and circumstances of your life. In the book and in the DVD of "The Secret", it explains how through the Law of Attraction, by simply thinking about and focusing on what you want you can attract all of the good that you want into your life. I wish that it was that simple. As I will explain in a moment, it is a little more too it than that. Well, quite frankly it's way more to it than that! But that's okay because we all have to start somewhere.

There is a part in the DVD of "The Secret" which I enjoyed and found very interesting is when one of the entrepreneur contributors of "The Secret" relates the story where he got into the habit of creating a "vision board". A "vision board"? A "vision board" is taking, for example, a 20' x 30" piece of white foam board and pasting photos and images of the cars, houses, money, clothes, or soul mate that you would like to attract in your life. The procedure is to look at this "vision board" just before going to bed at night and just after waking up in the morning while visualizing and *feeling* that all of these things depicted on your "vision board" are happening to you right now. (The *feeling* part of this exercise is most important.) The idea is that if you get the experience into your mind and heart, you will thus begin to attract these things into your life *effortlessly*. The effortless implication is where most people *will* get into trouble with this practice. Effort *is* required.

Below is an illustration of a "vision board".

Figure 1 This is a "vision board" that I created for myself.

"Faith has to do with things that are not seen, and hope with things that are not in hand."–Saint Thomas Aquinas

Now, back to my example of the entrepreneur in the DVD "The Secret." He related the story that he got in the habit of creating "vision boards" of the things, people, places, and circumstances that he wanted to attract into his life. Amongst the various images that he had pasted on this "vision board" were cars, soul mate, and clothes; he had also pasted a picture of a very nice mansion that was part of his vision. The scene changes, and he is in a room with his very young son while he is writing and doing other adult things. He has half opened boxes all over the room as he is unpacking things from having moved from a prior house into this new home. His little son is seated on top of one of the boxes, banging on the the side of the box with the heel of his shoe in the monotonous, annoying, tap, tap, tap that kids can do when ever there is the emptiness of a quiet room. The conversation which ensues goes something like this:

Tap. Tap. Tap. The heel of the foot bangs the side of the box.

"Honey, would you stop making that noise, daddy is trying to concentrate." The kid stops, but his curiosity gets piqued by this strange looking board with all of these interesting pictures on it.

"What's this, daddy?"

"That's a 'vision board'". A puzzled look surfaces on the child's face.

"What's a 'vision board', daddy?"

"Well, honey, when daddy wants something to happen in his

life, he puts pictures of it on a 'vision board' like this one." Dad kneels on the side of his son and begins to cry.

"Why are you crying, daddy?"

"I am looking at this house in the picture that I had pasted on this board a long time ago, and I now realize that this house in the picture is the exact same house we are living in right now!ß I hadn't realized that we are now living in our dream house. I now realize that in all of the businesses that I have created that this is the process that I went through. At last, I finally understand..."

Wait! Hold the phone! Stop the tape!!!! Does anybody other than me see the obvious? Sure, his vision board was a *part* of the process toward the achieving of the goal of his dream home. But did anybody really catch the part where this man says "...Out of all the *businesses* that I have created..." This man did <u>not</u> achieve this dream house while working as a checker in a Walmart during the day, and then ran home and stared at his "vision board" all night until he fell asleep. This man also *did* whatever it took to create the *means* for his dream house to happen. I am willing to put some good money on the bet that he set goals, took risks, had setbacks, solved problems, did not procrastinate and continued until he was able to purchase his dream home.

My point is this, and the message of the book that you have in your hands is this – it is more than just the Law of Attraction that will lead you to live the ultimate life possible. The Law of Attraction is indeed a great law and an important one, but it is cooperative with the other 11 great laws of the Universe. (Yes, there are a total of 12 laws that you need to know about or the Law of Attraction will not work for you the way it is meant to be.) In chapter 1 which follows, it is with great excitement and anticipation that I present to you, as Paul Harvey used to say, "–the *rest* of the story."

"Faith in oneself...is the best and safest course." –Michelangelo

"You are not only who you are today but also who you choose to become tomorrow."–
Melvin Powers

Part I

The 12 Great Laws of Success

"You are not only who you are today but also who you choose to become tomorrow."–
Melvin Powers

CHAPTER

The 12 Great Laws of the Universe

The Law of Attraction is a great (and popular) law because of its instant appeal to that part of us that wants "something for nothing" or practically nothing. Yes, the "your wish is my command" concept which offers the idea of the Law of Attraction is a great hit with the vast majority of the population. There is nothing inherently "wrong" with this normal, natural human tendency. The only fact is that there are the <u>other</u> great laws, and there are many things that <u>you</u> can do to wittingly or unwittingly <u>get</u> <u>in</u> <u>the</u> <u>way</u> <u>of</u> and stop the Law of Attraction from working. One of the ways is forgetting some of the other 11 laws which I will present to you in a moment, and then give each law its deserved attention dedicating to it a complete chapter. The Law of Attraction is not supposed to be as easy as "You're wish is my command" and <u>then</u> you get <u>everything</u> you want without effort. Think about this for a moment. Do you <u>really</u> want <u>everything</u> you wish to appear? And do you <u>really</u> want it to appear <u>without</u> effort?

"Well begun is half done."–
Aristotle

The Twilight Zone Episode "A Nice Place to Visit"

When I first saw this original black and white TV episode of the Twilight Zone back on April 15, 1960, I was a young lad, but I was still strongly impacted by the deep philosophical message that imparted this classic Rod Serling production. This tale was written by Charles Beaumont who in my opinion was a far better writer than Rod Serling could ever wish to be, and who wrote some of the most poignant episodes that left you thinking afterwards for years to come. This episode was written for all of those who believe that if you had your own genie in the lamp, always ready and waiting to answer instantly your every whim and desire, at your beck and call, you would truly be happy.

The story opens when a career criminal, Rocky Valentine, is shot and killed by police officers. He later awakens apparently to his surprise unharmed by the violent encounter with the police. He is not in any pain, rather he feels comfortable and relaxed and in very pleasant surroundings in a room that is luxuriously appointed with all of the necessary accoutrements of good living. He is suddenly startled by the company of a pleasant servant, dressed in an elegant all-white suit, shoes and tie. He introduces himself as, Mr. Pip. Pip is played by the

Sebastian Cabot, known by his portly appearance and well-groomed beard.

"Who are you?" asks Valentine.

"I am, Mr. Pip, and I am here to grant you whatever you wish."

"You'se gotta be kiddin' me."

"Oh, no, to the contrary, Mr. Valentine. I am here to grant you whatever you desire."

"Wow! Then maybe there was something I did good in my life. Though I can't remember anything. Oh, well. Let's go outside."

"As you wish, Mr. Valentine."

They start walking along the street when Rocky spots a police officer standing on the street corner. He becomes incensed at the sight of him as his hatred of the police still reverberates inside of him since his last recollection of the police was at the wrong end their guns. He whispers in Mr. Pip's ear, one of his first wishes. Suddenly, the police officer is turned into a kid of about 8 years old, standing now on the street corner with an oversized adult police's uniform looking surprised and ridiculous as Valentine passes by laughing mockingly at the sight of the now humiliated police officer.

"That was great, Pip! What else can we do?"

"Whatever you wish, Mr. Valentine."

"See things as you would have them instead of as they are." –Robert Collier

"I've always wanted to win at the races. Lets go to the race track."

"Splendid," replies Pip.

Valentine places his bet on a long shot.

"Hey, Pip, look at that! My horse is coming up in the lead. Look! Look! It's out in front! Yow Whee! We won! We won!

"Lets go and cash in your ticket and pick up your money."

"Sure, Pip. Sure. This is great!"

A little tired of the race horse scene, Valentine suggests something else.

"Hey, Pip. I always wanted to win at craps. What say we go to a casino and try out our luck?"

"But of course, Mr. Valentine. But of course."

They arrive at the casino and request a table. Valentine gets a pair of dice. He places them in his hands, wiggles them back and forth making the characteristic rattling noise of the dice.

"Come on, baby. Daddy needs a new pair of shoes"

"A perfect 7!" calls the casino worker at the table. "You win, sir."

"How's that for luck, hey, Pippy? Let's try again."

"Go right ahead, Mr. Valentine."

"Another perfect 7! You win again!"

"Wow, this is getting a little monotonous. Hey, Pip, if I though the dice again, will I win again?"

"I think and think for months and years. Ninety-nine times the conclusion is false. The hundredth time I am right"–Albert Einstein

"But of course, Mr. Valentine. I am here to grant your every wish. If you like, I could make you lose the next time you throw the dice, just to make it interesting."

"No, no, that's not what I mean. Oh, let's just forget this."

"Would you like to go back to your room, Mr. Valentine?"

"Yeah, yeah. Let's bring over some broads!"

Mr. Valentine and Mr. Pip arrive to the luxury hotel suite. The bell rings and in comes the most gorgeous and voluptuous looking woman any man could imagine. She enters and is all over Mr. Valentine, serving him and catering to his every whim. She then looks up at Valentine with an alluring glance and says, "Is there anything else that I can do for you?" Valentine looks at her and suddenly to his own surprise becomes bored at the overindulgence and the predictability of everything that he wishes. Not being able to take any more of this non-relenting instant gratification, Valentine turns to Mr. Pip.

"Mr. Pip, everything is all great and all, being here in heaven, but I am becoming bored out of my mind by always having everything whenever I want and knowing that whatever I do I will always win! I know that this may sound like a little strange request, but just for a change of pace, to make things a little bit more interesting, can you send me to the "other place"? referring to Hell.

Pip then lets out a bellowing reply, "The 'other place'?" Pip then begins to laugh in a villianous uproar. "This *is* the 'other place'!"

Valentine, in a sudden futile attempt tries to escape, but the door closes and locks. The demonic laughter of Pip echoes even louder as he mocks Valentine who realizes that this will be the life he is to live for all eternity.

So, the moral of this story is clear. You really in your heart of hearts do not want your life forever predictable, easy and indulgent of your every wish and whim. Have you ever thought about the psychology behind the person who *buys* jigsaw puzzles or who *enjoys* crossword puzzles. How much fun would it be if a computerized program at the push of the button put all of the jigsaw puzzles perfectly in place? How long could your attention be held playing a crossword game if the words all appeared on the paper as soon as you began. Look a little closer, and you will see, even with this simple example that this is how we are wired, all of us, as part of the human species. We *want* the challenge; we *want* to solve the mysteries. The problem arises when we mistakenly come to the conclusion that problems exists for some other reason–other than that of solving them! I believe that the game of life becomes too heavy, for so many people, because somewhere on the road they become convinced that they do not have the inner resources to play let alone win and enjoy this game we called life. I am here to spread the good news that you, me and everyone else is much grander and more powerful than any of us can imagine. That is in part the central theme and message of this book.

God Became So Bored That He Became You

I think that God, All-That-Is, the Universal Power, or whatever you would like to call the Ultimate and Infinite Creative Essence from whence all of us have come in His pre-form, pure consciousness state of beingness and self-awarness, had a peculiar problem that only God could have. Stay with me now. I know that not everyone will not be able to grasp, or least of all, accept want I am going to postulate here. If you disagree, just forgive me, and pass me off as a little nuts. It's okay, I can handle it. Let's get back to my postulation. God as He existed before the universe was created was in a pure formless state of having instantly everything He wished because He was/is the All. So everything God could wish, He *is* <u>already</u> that by the nature of His being All-That-Is. In essence, God was bored out of His mind in being and knowing all. So, to solve His problem, he decided to willingly forget who He was/is and divide Himself infinitely in the personalities of all humankind, past, present and future, and allow the fun to begin through each one of us on our individual paths of self-discovery <u>back</u> to our exciting true nature which is the very stuff of God. When we realize our true potential and special gifts and talents, we allow God to experience Himself joyously through us, and through alignment with His power and our belief in the power of God-in-you, we can indeed experience the joy to be, do and have anything that we choose in this wonderful event we call life.

The way back to the experience of your God-Presence within you is in the understanding and mastery of **The 12 Great Laws of the Universe.**

"Life is too short to read bad books." –Charles Prosper

Law #1 The Law of Goal Setting

This is the first great law which is basically the law of knowing what you want and setting clear mental and written goals. Once you have set a firm goal, you have asked or made your request to the Universe.

Law #2 The Law of Belief

The foundation of success and achievement will always be found in the principle of believing. *"As a man thinks in his heart, so is he."* The essence of believing is *feeling*, and that feeling is *believing*. There is great power and attractive force in the power of belief.

Law #3 The Law of Positive Expectation

Positive attitude and expectancy are one of the great keys to manifesting what you want in life. In life you truly get what you expect. If you

Law #4 The Law of Detachment
The Law of Detachment usually goes by another name that we are more familiar with and that it Faith. Faith is the ability to not worry over the results, but to know that the results are on its way.

Law #5 The Law of Attraction
The Law of Attraction is one of the most attractive laws because it appeals to the genie-in-a-bottle concept. This is the law which states simply, what you think about and focus on, you attract.

Law #6 The Law of Planning
This law tells you to start where you are and do what you can on the path to the achievement of your goals. Planning can be mental, but it is even more effective if it is written.

Law #7 The Law of Willingness to Do
The willingness to do whatever is necessary is that which lubricates the mechanics of inspired ideas.

"We cannot direct the wind, but we can adjust the sails."–Anonymous

Law #8 The Law of Immediate Action
The Universe rewards action. When you have an inspired idea, you must not procrastinate. You act on it immediately.

Law #9 The Law of Persistence
Life will give you anything that you desire if you insist on it, if you take every obstacle as a challenge in the way the person enjoys putting the pieces together of the jigsaw puzzle. It's all a game. Truly it's all a game. Have fun with it.

Law #10 The Law of Money
Money too comes to you based on clearly defined laws. You must know how to bless money, enjoy money, organize money, save money, invest money and give money properly to at last know true abundance.

Law #11 The Law of Gratitude
The Law of Gratitude works to put you in touch with the Creative Source that has given you all you have. You employ this great law before and especially after you have received what you have intended.

Law #12 The Law of Giving
The Law of Giving means giving to others especially in the way of helping and giving service to those less fortunate, for giving completes the circle. God gives to the giver and takes from the taker.

"You are not only who you are today but also who you choose to become tomorrow."–
Melvin Powers

CHAPTER 2

The Law of Goal Setting

Knowing what you want is the first step to getting what you want through The Law of Goal Setting. This is a two-fold process. You ask, that is, vibrate your wish and intention of what you want to see manifest to that which we may call Creative Intelligence or God by <u>setting</u> the goal and <u>feeling</u> the reality of that goal right now. All requests move via the communication of your <u>feeling</u> about a thing. Quite literally feeling is believing, and you will see it when you feel it. And feel it, you must, over and over, day after day with faith, joy and anticipation. There are essentially two ways that you can set a goal. You can do it mentally or written. Writing your goal down on and index card and reading it out loud once in the morning and once just before retiring to bed at night while seeing and feeling the reality of it in your mind as though it were already here in your experience is an excellent way to get the ball rolling and the creative ideas flowing that will give you the road map and perfect plan that will allow your dream to become reality.

Why You <u>Must</u> Have Goals

A man without a goal is like a ship without a rudder. I think that you would agree that if you got inside of a motor boat with no guiding rudder in a harbor, rebbed it up and let it go wheresoever, once it took off into the open waters the chances of crashing into the rocks, capsizing or smashing into another boat would be the very likely fate of such a foolish disembarkment. But isn't this exactly what we do with our lives when we go along day-by-day hoping that something better will happend to us or at least nothing worse in life will befall us. This is called living by default. Living by default assumes that there is nothing that you *can* do to make your life better. And if you <u>*know*</u> what you can do and don't do it, you life is no better than a person who doesn't know.

Goals work as does the magnifying glass. Place a piece of paper on the sidewalk in the bright sun on a clear summer day. Stand there for about an hour or two and see what happens. Assuming that you secured the paper to the ground with a weight on the edge of it, it will still be there, little warmer perhaps, but unchanged. Now take out a magnifying glass and point it onto the center of the paper and pull the magnifying back a little, and just a little more, until the light spot that

"Your success is only as good as the excuses you refuse to live by."–Charles Prosper

is beamed onto the paper begins to sizzle within seconds and thus burns a hole through it. The magnifying glass takes the rays of the sun and concentrates it onto the paper such that now those same warm sun rays can do things that it could not until it was concentrated. Thus is the power of goals. Goals are the magnifying glass which take the infinite powers of your mind and concentrate them with such power that they can burn and cut through any obstacle set before it. There is nothing more powerful than a made up mind with a goal at the forefront.

    I first heard the following example by the great motivational speaker, Zig Ziglar, and I want to give you my synopsis of it. Let us take the world's greatest archer, someone who, say, could hit a bullseye 10 out of 10 times from a hundred yards away with a bow and arrow. I can show you a way to outshoot this professional archer even though you have never picked up a bow and arrow. How? you say. Easy. Just blindfold this archer, spin him around a few times, and ask him to shoot. Sounds silly doesn't it. You are surely asking yourself right now. "How can he hit a target he can't even see?" Well, I have an even better question for you. "How can *you* hit a target that you don't even have?" You **must** have your goals.

    Now there is another trap that you can fall into. Some people confuse activity with accomplishment. Some load up there lives with all sorts of insignificant time-wasting activities that they literally crowd out the days of their lives making it impossible to achieve anything significant. You must first know and define what is important to you. Then you must start about with plans and steps to its accomplishment. (More on this a little later in this chapter.) Do you know what a processionary caterpillar is? It is a furry little caterpillar which follows unquestionably the caterpillar in front of it. The assumption is that the first caterpillar in the line (and somethings there may be dozens of caterpillars following eachother) knows where the food is or is at least the one on alert and looking for it. A scientist, tried an experiment. He found a row of processionary caterpillars traveling along a woods trail. He directed the first caterpillar to follow the back of the last caterpillar until all of the caterpillars formed a perfect circle, following eachother round and round and round. He put some pine needles, food for caterpillars, in the middle of the circle. The caterpillars followed eachother in circles for hours, days, until they all literally dropped dead from exhaustion when the goal, the food, the pine needles was right in their midst. When you do not set your own agenda, that is, set and follow your own goal, you become swept away by the agenda and thinking of the masses. Without a goal, you become just like the processionary caterpillar, doing what others do, going where others go and having what others have. If I stopped you right now and ask you what is you primary goal in life, could you tell me without hesitation? In order to

"All you need is a plan, a road map and the courage to press on to your destination."–Earl Nightingale

not become the human processionary caterpillar, you must discover your life purpose and set your life goal.

How to Discover Your Life Purpose

This is a big one for a lot of people. "If I only knew what my life purpose was, I most surely would pursue it!" Once you seriously set yourself on the path of seeking and searching for your life purpose, you have automatically placed yourself amongst the top 5% of the most enlightened individuals of society. To find your life purpose is the most important decision any human being can make. In finding your life purpose, you also answer other very deep and profound questions that scholars and sages have pondered all throughout the ages: "Who Am I?" "Where did I come from?" "Where am I going?"

Discovering and following your life purpose is the key to your experience of heaven on earth. Why? Because at the core of your life is your joy. Because the joyful doing of anything lies in using some facet of a God-given talent or gift that you have always known secretly in your heart but not done due to a negative mindset.

Whatever be your secret dream, wish or envision, you most certainly can obtain it, or the wish would have never been placed first in your heart. Then, why don't people achieve their goals? People don't achieve their goals because they don't <u>set</u> any goals, firmly or long enough in their minds on which to take action.

If you don't truly have everything that you really want, I'm going to tell you right now why not. Answer the following question by filling in the blanks:

"I would like to (state your goal), but...

a) (State first 'but'.)
b) (State second 'but'.)
c) (State third 'but'.)
d) (State fourth 'but'.)
e) (State fifth 'but'.)"

Whenever you don't achieve what you want, it is always because, somewhere, somehow along the line, you let your "but" get in the way. And the "but" that's in the way is always *your* "but".

If we are not achieving our goals, or if we are not in the process, or on the path of following our heart's true desires, we must ask ourselves, "<u>What</u> is it that I am not <u>willing</u> to do at present?" <u>Honestly!</u> Are you saying, "I can't afford to pursue my purpose because...

a) ...I might fail, and I would not be able to support myself."
b) ...I don't have enough money to start."

"Your life is only as good as the people you serve."–
Charles Prosper

c) ...I'm just too *'busy'* doing other things." Or,
d) ...Any *"good"* excuse which is a <u>bad</u> reason not to start."

Purpose vs. Goals

Many people sometimes confuse and believe that a <u>*purpose*</u> is the same as a <u>*goal*</u>. This is not the case. A purpose is a direction, and a goal is one of many specific ways of going in that direction. For example, going west is a <u>*direction*</u>, and this we might similiarly call a <u>*purpose*</u>. However, flying from New York to Seattle, driving from Florida to San Diego, or hitch-hiking from Detroit to Portland, would all be considered <u>*goals:*</u> all are different ways but with the same direction or purpose of <u>*going west*</u>. Goals may change, but purpose is permanent. Your purpose was assigned and designated to you from the day you were born. This is the thrust or direction that you unconsciously find yourself taking over and over again, all throughout your life, as a result of the way your hidden gifts and talents are silently guiding you. There are certain things and activities that you enjoy and just do well naturally. This is the direction of your purpose. The way you fulfill your purpose may take on the appearance of many different jobs, occupations, hobbies and careers until you find the vehicle that will take you in the direction of your purpose by the most direct, scenic and satisfying route.

Do what you love and nothing else, and the success and the money will follow. Follow your bliss. Your bliss is your joy. Your joy is what you love doing. What you love doing is what you do naturally. What you do naturally is consciously or unconsciously the exercise of a special gift or talent which you possess. Your special gift or talent when channeled to and focused on a specific goal becomes the key to never-ending success and happiness in your life.

Goals Are The Many Paths of Your Life Purpose

Quite simply, a goal is a specific route or detailed plan of a journey, an itinerary if you wish, expressed as a certain job, career, profession or business which is chosen in the way it points along the path of our never-ending, life-long purpose which is based on our talents and gifts, essentially who we are and who we must become, if we allow it to be as it was imprinted upon us from the day we were born. We tend to automatically express our life purpose through various jobs, careers, professions and business opportunities on an ever-increasing upward spiral of growth through greater and greater challenges and subsequently greater and greater achievements. There is no once and forever goal or opportunity that will necessarily suit you perfectly now until the end of your life with absolutely no change, growth or expansion. Over the course of his or her lifetime, a person, for example, may be a gardener, a worker for an environmental protection group, a writer, a politician

"Genius is an infinite capacity for taking pains."–
Jane Ellis Hopkins

and/or business entrepreneur, all during different phases of his or her life, and though these activities or goals are different, still be consistent with his or her purpose. The question to ask yourself is: What is the most logical thing that I should be doing now, or at least striving to do based on my current or past life experiences, and what are the strongest yearnings that I now hold in my heart?

The Transformational Power of a Goal

There is a certain irony in the reaching of a goal. The achievement of a goal is not nearly as important as the process which took you there. As a result of achieving a goal, you have become a new person. You had to overcome obstacles, challenges and stumbling blocks of all kinds. In order to do this, you had to develop new skills, new strengths, new perspectives, new insights, new knowledge and new wisdom. Had you not had a goal to achieve, none of this could ever have happened.

When you reach for a goal, follow your dreams, meet and overcome the challenges that stand in your way, realize it or not, you have been skillfully trained with weights, pulleys and stairclimbing in Life's spiritual fitness center by the greatest Master Trainer of all.

The Processional Effect

When you strive and move toward a goal, your experience is much like the processional effect of the honeybee. The honeybee instinctually has a goal. The goal is to gather as much nectar as possible from flower to flower. Nectar gathering may be the ostensible goal, but in the process of its objective, this honeybee unwittingly achieves the pollination of the flowers necessary for the growth of new blossoms and new flowers. So a goal is not important because you achieve it but because of what it makes you become. A goal is nature's way of making you become more. The law of life is evolutionary. The law of life is that you must always become more. This is why when a goal is reached, another and probably greater goal is usually embarked upon. Life always seeks to grow and expand through *you*, ever more and ever more.

Before you go off and embark upon a new career in a new field or before you seek out a new business opportunity, examine very closely first the job, profession or work you are now doing, that is, the profession or industry where you have had the majority of your life experience. I am not saying that you must continue down the same old trodded path, but only make sure that you are not walking away from an obvious new start in a field that you already know and have a place. Everything that you have experienced and have learned up until now has been the platform for your next step upward. There are no accidents in a perfectly ordered universe of laws of cause and effect. You have experienced everything that you have up until now as the necessa-

"Mediocrity knows nothing higher than itself, but talent instantly recognizes genius." –Arthur Conan Doyle

ry preparation for your next important steps of growth whatever they may be.

There is a funny thing about the conscious selection of a goal when none is obvious at the moment. Goals tend to seek _you_ out. What I mean is that oftentimes upon the commencement of a particular goal, through a series of unexpected events and so-called coincidences, you are led to something much better than you ever dreamed of. But what is for sure, you must chose a goal and start somewhere. Anything worth doing is worth doing lousy. Just choose something – _anything_! Make corrections later.

Choosing A Worthwhile Goal

Success is the progressive realization of a worthwhile goal. For a goal to be worthwhile, it must serve and improve the quality of life of others. Therefore, if you have a worthy goal, and if you are actively and progressively engaged in the step-by-step pursuit of it, serving others, _enjoying_ the challenges and triumphs along the way, be you in the beginning, middle or final stages of its achievement, you _are_ by definition a _success_. Later money becomes your physical scorecard as to how well you are doing on the material level if that has happened to be part of your goal as well.

"There's a way to do it better...find it."–Thomas Edison

Discovering Your Purpose Through Serving Others

I have people very frequently ask me, "Charles, but how can I find my true purpose?" If it is your purpose, it automatically becomes true. I have at last found an easy, sure-fire answer to this all-consuming question by the searcher of truth and light. Just look around in your immediate life right now and ask, "What is it that I can do to provide the most _service_ to others?" Let me repeat that question again, because if you can grasp its significance, you will never worry about your purpose, how to make a living nor not having enough money and prosperity ever again. "What is it that I can do to provide the most _service_ to others?" Start right here with this question, and _keep looking for_ the perfect ocupational, profession or business opportunity vehicle that will allow you to give more and greater ways to give service to others using you particular training, talents, gifts and personal life experience. The purpose of _everyone's_ life on the planet, when you think about it deeply and profoundly, is the answer to "How can I give more service to others with who I am, what I know, where I've been and where I could go." Make you life about giving and serving others, and your true purpose will be effortlessly and obviously revealed to you. This I promise you.

Why Do You Exist?

In life, you get the right answers, if you ask the right questions. Why do you exist? Have you ever seriously asked yourself that question? The most superficial and obvious answer would be that your parents got together, conception took place, and you were born. But upon seeking answers beyond the sexual communion of our mother and father, we begin to intuitively sense without the necessity of some scientific proof that – we came from somewhere and we are going somewhere. From the apparent nothingness when we arrive in a tiny body, family and friends look at us and wonder what will the future bring, or correctly what will _we_ bring to the future. I would submit to you that you exist to allow God to give - _though you_ - to _others_, and when God passes _though_ you, you feel bliss, joy and spiritual satisfaction. This is what is meant by follow your bliss, and success follows you.

There Are No Accidents

There is no such thing as chance, luck, accident or coincidence. For being unable to discern an immediate cause or connection of any given occurence, our human ego demands an explanation even if it means calling something a "coincidence." We as humans tend to label things we don't understand thus giving ourselves a false sense of having explained it. We live in a universe of law and order. Did you know that mathematically speaking no one has ever been able to scientifically prove _randomness_, that is, that it is possible for something to completely and totally happen by chance? They have come very close, but it never has been proven without a shadow of doubt. What is it that keeps a planet in orbit, never colliding with another planet? What is it that keeps millions upon millions of planets all throughout the universe in orbit and never colliding with eachother. What intelligence could a planet possess where it would know exactly at what axis to turn day after day, month after month, year after year, and always stay on track? The same law or force that governs the orbit of the planets orders also the course of purpose of our lives with the same precision, with the same harmony and with the same masterful orchestration as seen in the infinite wonder and manifestation of this daily miracle we call life.

Everything Has a Purpose

Let us suspend for a moment the usual left brain, "if-I-can't-see-it-then-I-don't believe-it" skepticism and assume that this is indeed a world of law and order and there are no accidents; then everything in existence must have a purpose. Then, at that moment of realization of the purposefullness of everything in the universe, you too become like a planet whirling majestically in space, on track, in orbit and on purpose. Why would the universe do for the stars and planets what it wouldn't do for you, God's most precious creation?

"Be like the eraser...forever forgiving." –Charles Prosper

We Need You

Do you know that all of humanity awaits you? You are very, very special. So special are you that mankind has only one chance to receive what you have come here to give. Never have the likes of you in all of your multi-faceted possibilities been seen before in all of history. Though gifts similar to yours may have been given before, yours has never appeared exactly the way only you will be able to deliver it. If you withhold it and never strive to uncover and develop all of your latent potential, all of us will lose out, for there will never be another exactly like you. Nature never repeats itself – not even a leaf or fingerprint, no matter how many times billions upon billions of leaves or fingerprints appear on the earth. Once a creation is made, it is never repeated again in exactly the same way.

You Are Unique (An Endangered Species)

By reason of your uniqueness, and by the fact that you are a once-in-a-lifetime event, someone who may leave us before parting eternal treasures, you immediately become classified on the endangered species list. If you were not absolutely necessary to complete the process of creation, you would have never been born. Universal creation is on an on-going infinite mission of expansion, including the necessary possibility of expansion through you.

"Fact is a disguise of faith." –Charles Prosper

Giving: The Reason of All Life Purpose

Giving is the best definition of love. What most people call love really amounts to some form of addiction. 'I love chocolate." "I love music." "I love you." Giving is the best definition of love with no strings attached. The very essence of the universe and nature is that of abundant giving. Look at the forest. Look at the starts. Look at people. If giving truly is love then we become love in action by giving. That's why *for*giving works so well when we master it. Forgiving is a type of giving, that is, you give *for* or give *in the place of*. Someone gives you anger, and you *give* understanding *in place of* or *for* (the anger). You give-for, or, as we know it, you *for*-give.

It is a known fact that mothers who have decided to nurse their babies, <u>must</u> give their milk. The breast will fill up with milk so fast until the milk will stretch the skin of the breast so tightly that it will hurt the mother if the milk is not given to the baby quickly. The compulsion of life's need is to give unto itself. That is why when we give to others in some way, we are giving at the same time to ourselves. We learn something best when we teach it (give it). When a tree is overloaded with fruit, the tree will be compelled to release it (give it), and fruit will drop from its branches and fall on the ground as an offering. With the issue of choosing out life purpose, we are not important for what we have chosen to do but rather are important for what and how we have chosen to give.

Stewards and Not Owners

What can we claim as ours that was not previously given to us first? By the nature of the fact that the universe has given us all that we have had from birth, at best, we may only consider ourselves as administrators of these possessions, places and things of our life experiences to the degree that we can enhance them and add to them. We can only be stewards in spite of all of the self-deluding ego demands of the human psyche that would like us to believe otherwise. What can we truly own that will not one day have to be given up?

Everything Is On Loan

Know that you cannot *own* anything. Everything in life is on loan to you: your body, your clothes, your house, your wife or husband, your children, your job, your money – *everything*. You cannot own anyone's behavior no matter how bad they act. You cannot even own your own present age–for it you are 39 today, next year you will have to give it up for age 40. This is a statement that all in life changes, and nothing stays the same. All changes because the message is that nothing is ours, and by its nature, the universe must always create anew and evolve into higher and higher levels of expression–through you. Therefore, if the whole thrust of life is on giving, does it not make sense for us to divest ourselves of the quest for having, hoarding, getting and owning, and focus more of our time and energy on contributing to, enhancing and giving to all that which we would have ourselves to believe we can own?

If you would be one and move in harmony with the life energy of all that is, you must embrace in its totality that your life and all life is, has been and will always be centered around how well you can serve and improve the quality of life by giving what you have to give and thus, as an unavoidable result, reap the peace, pleasure and prosperity of perfect living for yourself.

So when you ask, ask that you will be shown the path of how to give more to others and thus more to yourself. Your goals must a purpose. Your purpose, if you trust what you already know in your heart but may have doubted for so long, you will be shown which goal to set first. Assuming now that you understand your purpose, to give of the uniqueness of who and what you are, and assuming that you have decided upon a specific goal as the first step toward fulfilling your purpose, let us now look at a proven and scientic formula for setting and achieving any and all goals that you seek that are worthy of you and which are not set to harm anyone. I would like to now show you The 7-Step Goal Setting Success Formula.

"The mind is the limit. As long as the mind can envision the fact that you can do something, you can do it, as long as you really believe 100 percent."–Arnold Schwarzenegger

The 7-Step Goal Setting Success Formula

This fabulous formula for setting and achieving goals, I learned from one of my greatest teachers, Zig Ziglar. This goal setting success formula has been tested and proven by countless successful people all the world over. Now it's your turn. Here is it.

Step #1 Write Down Your Goal.

Step #2 Write Down When You Expect to Obtain the Goal.

Step #3 Write Down Obstacles in the Way of Your Goal.

Step #4 Write Down the Needed People and Organizations

Step #5 Write Down A Plan of Action.

Step #6 Write Down What You Need to Know or Learn.

Step #7 Write Down *Why* This Goal is Important to You.

One thing you will immediately notice about this list is that each step of the 7-Step Goal Setting Success Formula starts with the words "Write Down..." The reason for this is that written goals are committed goals and mental goals become wishful thinking and whims for many people. I have even heard it say that a wish becomes a goal at the point it is written down. Also by writing everything down, this allows you to look at the entire process with a calm, analytical and rational eye, something like the scientist who embarks upon a mission of discovery and takes everything that happens as new data to proceed further. A true scientist sees no failure but only observes results; he records data and changes his or her approach until the discovery or the objective has been reached. By writing everything down, you will truly have a roadmap to the fortune and fulfillment that you seek. When was the last time you've seen a pirate seach for a treasure without a map? Let's take each of the seven steps and look at them closely one by one.

Step #1 - Write Down Your Goal

Before we start, let me make a suggestion of organization. Get yourself a 3-ring binder the type that have the clear plastic sheet on the fron cover and back cover for the purpose of sliding in a sheet of paper that identifies the subject of the notebook. On your computer, type out a sheet with large letters that say, "My Goal Achievement Notebook". Make sure that you type your name on the front as well. Put in it about 100 lined, loose leaf sheets of paper, and we are ready to begin.

"The tragedy of life doesn't lie in not reaching your goal. The tragedy lies in having any goal to reach."–
Benjamin Mays

This goal achievement notebook will serve as a journal and record of your progress. You will, along the way, write in entries of what is working and what is not. If something is working, just do more of it. If something is not working, then calmly observe that, record what that is, change your approach, then try something different. It is really just as simple as that. Remember, men don't fail, they only stop trying.

On you very first sheet, write on the top the heading in bold letters, "My Goal". Write in a clear statement a goal which might look something like this.

"By December 12, 201_ , I intend to own and operate a private elementary school which teaches and emphasizes positive self-image psychology, goal setting and the principle of believing in oneself. I intend that this school operate profitably and be the touchstone of over a 100 charter schools that I will create all over the country."

"Aim at nothing, and you will succeed."–Anonymous

Now, let me give you another tip of writing down your goal. Not only must you write it down in your 3-ring binder goal achievement notebook, but you must also write down your goal on *two separate small index cards,* say 3" x 5". The purpose of this is to paste one of these cards on your bathroom mirror where you will have to see it every day that you get dressed in the morning and as you are brushing your teeth just before you go to bed at night. The purpose of the other index card is to carry it around with you during the day to look at and think about as much as possible. I like to use the index card for bookmarks inside of a particular book on success and motivation that I might happen to be reading at the time. The goal cards that I carry around with me today, I print up on business cards on my computer and carry them around even more conveniently and discreetly in my wallet.

Step #2 - Write Down When You Expect to Obtain the Goal

I am sure that what became apparent to you was the part of setting a target date for the achievement of your goal after reading your sample goal statement in the above section. You must have a target date and a target objective to get your creative juices following to work on something that is specific, definitive and achievable. Try to place a date with in the parameters of reasonable possibility. If you are going to buy a million dollars of real estate and at present you only have $567.00 in the bank, it is probably best that you not put the target date for sometime next week but rather some time in the next 3 to 5 years. Each situation is, of course, different. You want the goal-setting process be a means to solving your problems. You don't want the goal-setting process to become a problem in itself. There is one last part of reading your goal card every morning as you start your day and every night just before you retire. It is most important that you see, with your eyes opened or closed, and _**feel**_ that whatever it is that you have set as your goal is already happening in your experience right now! Feeling has a lot to do with the Law of Attraction which we will cover in detail in a later chapter.

Step #3 - Write Down the Obstacles in the Way of Your Goal

Surely you did not believe that you we just going to set a goal, create a plan and achieve your goal with no problems or setbacks. There will be problems or setbacks. Expect them. Identify and write down what you anticipate to be some of your challenges when you start. You may already know why you have procrastinated on starting what you have know is you want to do. Unconsciously, you know what some of those initial obstacles are, which is the reason why you have put it off so much. Write it out on paper. Identifying those things that you fear most and then writing them down will reduce most of their paralyzing power. Now you are approaching your challenges like a true scientist on a mission of discovery.

Step #4 - Write Down the Needed People and Organizations

"I start where the last man left off." –Thomas Edison

Very few of us achieve many truly great things in life without the help of others. Remember that no matter what problem, challenge or goal that you have set for yourself, you can rest assured that someone has been through almost the identical situation and has learned how to solve it. This someone may be in the form of a mentor, a group dedicated to what you are trying to achieve as might it be an organization or an association. Let us not forget about formal training. We live now in the information age and there is a wealth and plethora of means to getting answers to whatever it is that we seek. There are community education courses, short courses that might run as little as a 3-hour workshop, or as much as several months. The key idea is this, you are looking for a mentor. Whoever it is that is teaching the course or whoever it is that heads the group or organization in your particular field, approach that person. First offer to pay him or her a consultation fee to become your mentor. You will be surprised how many times many experts, when they like you, will not even want to charge you if they can just see that you are earnest, sincere, and determined to succeed and are willing to follow through with their guidance. I know that this is a fact from first hand experience. Multi-millionaire mail order guru, Melvin Powers of the Wilshire Book Company in Chatsworth, CA back in 1986, took me under his wing and taught me everything that I know about book publishing, promoting seminars in community colleges, as well as getting on the internet when the whole idea was still new and encouraged me to create my first web site. Because of his guidance, I learned what it was like to create a six-figure income. I remembered when I first walked into his office back in October of 1986.

"Mr. Powers, I would very much like to get my book published, so I would like to know how I would go about making a formal submission to you in order for that to happen?"

"Just call me, Melvin, please. Well, Charles, your book in on a specialty and a niche of professional balloon decorating which does not fall in the line of any of the books that I publish which cover success and motivation, like "Think and Grow Rich" by Napoleon Hill of which I sold 5 million copies and "Psycho-Cybernetics" by Maxwell Maltz which sold 7 million copies. I would suggest, rather than have me publish it and give you a small 5% in royalties, publish it yourself and keep 100% of the profit. I know of many people who become very successful as self-publishers. You could be the next."

"Wow, that sounds good to me. How might I get started?"

"First purchase my book on self-publishing entitled, 'How to Self-Publish Your Book and Have the Fun of Being a Best-Selling Author' written by yours truly."

"Can I get it from you right now?"

"Of course, shall I gift wrap it for you," he says with a smile.

"No, I'll consume it without a wrapper." We both laugh, and that was the start of a friendship that has lasted until this day of 2012. You can visit Melvin Powers web site at:

`http://www.mpowers.com`

I also just recently had a similar experience when I decided to become a serious real estate investor. (We are also talking about the Law of Attraction here as well.) On my birthday on October 2, 2006, I decided that it was about time for me to become seriously, really serious about starting a plan of real estate investment. I was on a plane trip back to Los Angeles from seeing relatives during Christmas vacations a couple of months earlier. I am walking up the aisle of the plane. My seat is 4-F, near the window. It is a crowded flight. There are a lot of people in the aisle, walking at a snail's pace, in a kind of half-step forward shuffle, bags and ticket in hand as they search for their assigned seats. Ah, there's mine! To the right. Three more seats ahead. I see a middle-aged gentleman, maybe in his sixties, gold framed glasses reading a magazine. To his left, seated in the middle is an attractive lady, fortyish, with the look of maybe someone from Sweden. She too is reading a magazine as I approach them to prepare myself to squeeze between both of them to make my way to the window seat.

"Excuse, me. That's my seat. May I squeeze through?" The gentleman reading the magazine smiles, stands and moves into the aisle

"Set short term goals and you will win games. Set long term goals, and you will win championships."–
Anonymous

allowing me to squeeze and grunt my way pass the lady in the middle who tries to move her two long legs to the side allowing me to pass over her knees.

"Thank you," I say to the lady.

"You're welcome."

It is a night flight, and we settle, in to maybe sleep or maybe try to read by the light of the tiny beam light overhead of each seat.

"Do you know how long the flight is?" I ask her.

"I think it is about 3 hours," she replies.

The gentleman seated at the aisle seat comments that he takes this flight back to Los Angeles from Costa Rica every month.

"Every month!" I reply. "What do you do in Costa Rica, if you don't mind my asking, every month?"

"I'm a real estate investor, and I have property in Costa Rica as well as here in the United States. And I get to go visit my estates and rental properties each month. It is the greatest life in the world."

My interest piques. The lady in the middle passively listens.

"How did you get involved in real estate investing?" I ask him.

"Well, I used to be a teacher, and I realized that I would not get anywhere in being able to enjoy the best that life as to offer by just doing that. So I decided to study and get a real estate sales license. I then sold real estate to save up the initial capital that I would need to start investing while at the same time being exposed to the industry of property purchase and values. In my sales office, I was lucky enough to have a mentor who taught me everything I needed to know to get started in real estate investing for which I have been doing now full-time for over 20 years."

"Talk about a coincidence," I say. "I too work as a substitute teacher, and I have come across the same conclusion that just teaching would never take me to the heights of my aspirations." The lady in the middle now speaks.

"I am an substitute teacher also," she declares. She intently listens as I begin to talk more with this interesting gentleman.

I extend my hand first to the lady. "My name is Charles."

Receiving my hand, "I'm Donna."

"I'm Raymond," replies our real estate investor.

"Raymond, you are doing exactly what I would like to do. I would be happy to pay you a consultation fee for you to become my mentor and show me how to become a real estate investor once we get back to Los Angeles."

"I tell you what, since I go back to Costa Rica every month, and since you told me that you are a Spanish teacher and interpreter, how 'bout you teach me Spanish and I teach you real estate as long as you buy lunch."

"Wisdom is knowing what path to take next...integrity is taking it." –Anonymous

"You got a deal," I say. And this was the beginning of my friendship and my real estate investment career with multi-millionaire real estate investor Raymond Sandstrom. Can you see the pattern here? Was it luck that I was able to attract my mentors at just the right place and the right time? Had I not set the goal first, I would have never even *asked* for help. When the student is ready, the teacher appears.

Step #5 - Write Down a Plan of Action

"Planning is Power." I forgot where I first saw or heard this, but this should become part of your success mottos. The thing that separates us from the animals is not only our ability to choose and use free will but also and more importantly is our ability to plan a course of action, a road map so to speak that will allow us to set course on the path of our destiny. Before I give you a very effective technique to beginning planning, let me say that a plan is alive. What I mean is that it is expansive and contractive. You should make plans but not *rigid* plans. The secret to planning is to start where you are and to think out and write down the first most *obvious* steps that you should take. With more experience and trying out this and that, you will find that your original plan may have to be modified. The rule is this, whatever you are doing and things get better and better, you are on the right track. Whatever you are doing that gets more and more difficult, you are on the wrong track, thus requiring you to change your approach. You plan of action oftentimes can and should be done with the help of your mentors or paid expert in your field of endeavor.

"Your happiness is just on the other side of your fears. Can you cross over?"–
Charles Prosper

Count to 20 for Plenty

We are still talking about the planning process here. I am assuming that you have read and studied all you could intially on your subject that involves your goal. I am also assuming that you have consulted with any and all truly qualified mentors about some of the best courses of action. Now it is time to do something which has lead to some of the most rewarding results all of my life. I first learn this technique from the world-renowned author and motivational speaker, Earl Nightingale. This essentially is a very effective method of what is popularly called "brainstorming" or thinking with your brakes off. Even though I have been doing this when I have needed to solve a problems for many, many years, it never ceases to amaze me at the surprisingly positive results and answers that I *always* get. It is even more amazing to me why so few people know about it, and even more so, why so few people who *do* know about it and have used it successfully on many occasions don't use it regularly to solve *all* problems when they arise. I would suggest that you get up an hour earlier before you start your day, and for 60 minutes everyday for the next 5 days practice this great problem- solving method.

Go out and purchase a special spiraled notebook that will be used exclusively and solely for the purpose of "brainstorming" and problem solving. Whenever you want to either solve a difficult problem or to come up with great ideas to begin the planning and road map of your goal, you will immediately and calmly go to your "Problem-Solving Notebook". Open to the first page, and write down on the top of the page, "My Goal is *(State the goal.)*" Or, as it may be the case, "The Challenge is *(State the problem.)*" Number vertically the page from 1 to 20; It will look something like this:

My Goal is to Earn $50,000 a Month by December 12, 2015

(Possible solutions that could work:)

1.
2.
3.
4.
5.
6.
7.
8.
9.
10.
11.
12.
13.
14.
15.
16.
17.
18.
19.
20.

"Many are stubborn in pursuit of the path they have chosen, few in pursuit of the goal."–Friedrich Nietzsche

Begin to write down the first thing that pops into your mind no matter how far-fetched or ridiculous it might seem to the rational, critical, analytical mind. You are writing now at a purely creatively level. You are tapping into the limitless possibility thinking of your subconscious mind where the seat of all "impossible" creation lies. Now, let me tell you what is going to happen. Most of your ideas will not be any good in the practical sense, but when you least suspect a truly surprisingly good and practical idea, worth testing will pop into you mind.

THE LAW OF GOAL SETTING

There is something else that will happen. You will start your mind rolling and working for you even when you are not actively practicing this technique every day for the first 5 days. You see, once the subconscious mind knows what it is that you are trying to achieve, it begins to work for you on automatic pilot 24 hours a day – even while you sleep and dream.

I can easily prove this to you by way of your own experience. Have you ever seen a person on the street some morning who recognizes you and remembers your name. She cheerfully greets you by name, but for the life of you, you just cannot remember hers. You are a little embarrassed to ask her her name because you feel that if she remembered yours, you should at least be able to return the courtesy and remember hers. You think, and you think, but the name, though on the tip of your tongue, just won't come to mind in that moment. You wish her farewell, and go about your business for the rest of the day. You are still a little disappointed that you were not able to remember her name. You think and think again, but still to no avail. So, you let it go. (You detach.)

"We will either find a way or make one." –Hannibal

It is 8:00 p.m., and you are about to step into the shower. "Elsa!" pops into your mind out of nowhere. Then you remember. The friend's name that you saw in the street today is named Elsa. Now, what happened during the time you consciously made the effort to remember, then let it go? The subconcious mind went into action to solve your problem and find the answer to the goal of who was the friend – even though you had left it alone and had begun to do something else totally unrelated. When it (the subconcious) found the answer, the name of the friend, it popped it into your conscious mind.

You may also get the answer while sleeping and wake up from a vivid dream with a perfect solution worth testing. I suggest to be a super-achiever and creative thinker to always, always, *always* keep a small note pad and pencil with you wherever you go and all throughout the day, and even at your bedside for you might awake from a vivid dream with the solution be able to *immediately* write it down.

I can only tell you from experience that if you are not ready to write down the inspiration or the dream immediately when it happens, you will forget it, and it will never come back to you the same. *That* brain child will have aborted and died forever. Be ready for all of your great ideas with a small notebook, one that you can put in the palm of your hand, and a pencil to write them down as soon as they tell you they are ready to be born. Sometimes I find myself pulling over to the side of a freeway to write down that "million-dollar idea" before it flirts and dissipates away. Start this creative process by counting to 20 and thinking on paper. Just the practice itself, while doing it gives you an incredible sense of well-being. You will need to try it a few times to understand what I mean. Once you start this practice as a habit, I am sure that you will keep it up for life. It's fun as well as it is exciting.

Step #6 - Write Down What You Need to Know or Learn

I had a student of one of my party-balloon-decoration business workshops call me and ask that I help her with some of the very basic steps of starting a business. She said that she didn't even know how to write up an invoice, or how to set up a DBA (doing business as) registry to open up a business checking account using the name of her business. I explained to her that what she needed was to look up the names of the community colleges in her area and get the catalog of the community education courses, which are short courses that are sometimes one evening or a couple of weekends for 3 hours a class, which teach a wide variety of subjects. I suggested that she look up a course on how to start a business which included all of the basic steps from selecting a business name, how to set and do bookkeeping, invoicing, marketing, etc. I told her that she would need to become information-hungry and seek out and take all the necessary courses, and read all of the necessary books, or listen to the necessary audio cassettes on the subject.

Let us not also forget that many of the necessary books and audio compac discs on the subjects that we need more information on can be found in the public library. After taking whatever course or courses that you have to take, go and get to know your instructor better. Ask him or her specific questions and advice on the particular thing that you are trying to do. Listen. Take note, and test those ideas that you feel could possibly work for you. If something you hear sounds really good, then go out and give it a try. If what you hear does not ring true or sound, then always trust your judgement, and decide not to do it, and move in a different direction. The idea is that you must keep yourself open and willing to learn and do whatever is necessary to achieve your goal.

Step #7 - Write Down *Why* This Goal is Important to You

One of the guarantors of perserverance in any goal is the clear understand as to why this goal is of importance to you. Do you need to make $500,000 a year to be able to send your daughter through medical school? Do you need to start that private school because you have the vision to teach positive self-image psychology and create a new generation of enlightened leaders of today's society? Do you need to become that actor, writer, poet, scientist or businessperson because you know that you will bring to the world a new wave of new light, love and joy? Do you need to do whatever it is that you have set out to do because in your heart you have *always* known that this has been your calling and your gift to humankind? Once you understand the *why,*

"He who has a <u>why</u> to live for can bear almost any <u>how</u>."–Friedrich Nietzsche

you will have place yourself in the powers of one of the other great laws, the Law of Willingness-to-Do which we will talk about at length in a later chapter.

What is the Meaning of Life?

I just can't leave this chapter without giving you an inspired moment one day when I was thinking on the subject of goals and the meaning of life. This is highly philosophical, but this is what came to me.

The meaning of life is the infinite journey of discovery to God which at the same time, but an essential discovery of ourselves. Through the discovery of our unique talents, we fulfill our purpose for which we were born and placed here on this earth for a designated and very limited amount of time. Our talents are not ours but are divine loans or instruments entrusted to us with which God, through us, may operate. He attempts to inspire us to give service to others with our talents. We, through our love of doing, will often times inspire others to also search for their own unique talents which, when found and given, will again bless the world and give meaning to its existence.

The positive signpost of finding one's purpose and correctly using one's talents is joy. The joy that we feel is but only the joy that God feels and shares with us at that very moment of its experience. Each person's joy, by example, thus inspires the next person who is ready to discover his or her joy and talents, and thus find the meaning of life through the divine discovery of God, self and the universe which is made again and again, on higher and higher levels, and all throughout the boundless planes of infinity.

"Solutions depend on how you define the problem."–
Charles Prosper

"You are not only who you are today but also who you choose to become tomorrow."–
Melvin Powers

CHAPTER 3

The Law of Belief

The Law of Belief is stated in the Scriptural quote "As a man thinketh in his heart, so is he." It has been said as in other ways. "You are what you think." The Law of Belief can also be called The Law of Feeling because what you believe, you *feel* to be true. And how you feel causes you to perceive the world in a certain way and causes you to act or react in a certain way which in turn causes a particular experience or result in your life. The type of belief that causes real change in your life be it positive or negative is the type of belief that you "think in your heart" or feel with intensity.

What Exactly is a Belief?

A belief is a feeling of certainty about a certain experience, idea, situation or observation. Your beliefs not only determine what choices you make and what you do, your beliefs also determine how your body will respond. In fact, one might say that our life experience is nothing but a well-organized belief system wrought and molded consciously or unconsciously by ourselves. "Anything the mind of man can conceive and believe can be achieved" was pronounced by Napoleon Hill in his classic work on prosperity, riches and success in the book "Think and Grow Rich" which, by the way, in my opinion, should be required reading in every public school starting as early as third grade. Not only Napoleon Hill, but sages all throughout history have unraveled and "discovered" the secret power of belief.

Faith and Belief Are Synonymous

Though it is usually within the circles of spiritual and religious discussion that we hear the word faith, but we are really hearing the synonym for belief. The essence of the concept and experience of faith or belief is the fact that it does not really require immediate external validation to work. What I mean is that once you truly believe in something and have the faith to do it, you will do it in a way that produces the thing that you believed but did not see. At 8-years old, my daughter Luzemily's favorite motto was "You'll see it when you believe it," first popularized by Wayne Dyer and his best-selling book of the same title. You become what you believe, and your environment, and even the people

"What we see depends mainly on what we look for."–John Lubbock

around you become what you believe. Whatever is your faith becomes your fate.

Thoughts Are Things

I have always loved that expression because it encapsulates a very important facet of our lives. If we become what we think about and if that which we think are our thoughts, then we must become vigilant in that which produces all thought, which is our mind. We must be careful what thought-seeds we allow to fall into the fertile ground of our minds. The strange thing is that thoughts, beliefs and our faith in things are born out of the thought-seeds that fall consciously or unconsciously into our minds over a period of time to take root and bear the fruit of through experience these particular thought or thoughts. We get thought-seeds thrown into our minds from our parents. We get thought-seeds thrown into our minds from the news. We get thought-seeds thrown into our minds from the company that we keep, the things that we read, the movies we see and the music that we habitually listen to. The bad news is that if we let the type of thought-seeds that fall into our minds be random from the world mind then for the most part we will be receive mostly the negative type or at best just the *ordinary* thought-seeds that the world has to offer. The good news that if we *choose* good thoughts, happy thoughts, successful thoughts, peaceful thoughts, loving thoughts, confident thoughts, forgiving thoughts, prosperous thoughts, healthty thoughts, money thoughts and fun thoughts, then this will be our experience. Why? Because thought encapsulates the belief. Belief produces the feeling, and feeling creates the action. Action produces the experience, and experience becomes the fruitful harvest of our mental agriculture. We choose the thoughts that we think by the books we read, the audio tapes that we listen to, the company that we keep and the meditation that we practice. (More on meditation in a later chapter.)

"Something will turn up."–
Bejamin Disraeli

What the Sages Have to Say About the Power of Belief

Throughout the centuries, many camps of philosophical thought have argued on the minuscia of many concepts, but there has been on one point that all of been in complete and unanimous agreement, and that is —we become what we believe. Here are what some of the wisest men over the centuries have said about the importance and power of faith and belief in yourself:

"All that we are is a result of what we have thought."
–Buddha

"Whether you think you can or think you can't, either way you are right."–Henry Ford

"What things soever ye desire, when ye pray, believe that ye receive them, and ye shall have them."–Mark 11:24

"A man's life is what his thoughts make of it."–Marcus Aurelius

"A man is what he thinks about all day long."–Ralph Waldo Emerson

"If you think like a winner, you become a winner."–Melvin Powers

"You'll see it when you believe it."–Wayne Dyer

"The greatest discovery of my generation is that human beings can alter their lives by altering their attitudes of mind."–William James

"Be thou faithful unto death."–Revelations 2:10

What You Say is What You Get

Now, you may ask, "How do I best control my beliefs?" There are many good techniques for keeping a watchful guard over what goes into and out of your mind which are your thoughts. The most immediate handle onto your thinking is what you say to others, and especially what you say to *yourself*. Be very careful of the use of the word "I am". Whatever you state after you say "I am" becomes a self-fulling prophesy. Saying, "I am a winner" produces one type of thought, feeling, action and result, and saying such things as, "I am a loser" produces another type of thought, feeling, action and result. Like thoughts attract like experiences. Your world soon becomes a mirror of your thinking by what you say to yourself about yourself. Believe and accept that you deserve the best, and the best will surely become a part of your experience.

"You are not only who you are today but also who you choose to become tomorrow."–
Melvin Powers

CHAPTER 4

The Law of Positive Expectation

"You may be disappointed if you fail, but you are doomed if you don't try."–
Beverly Sills

A person is gravely ill with a rare form of lymphatic cancer. He is given one month to live by doctors due to the advanced stages of his condition. A new doctor walks into the office.

"Mr. Rentería, I have good news for you," says Dr. Goldman with an air of enthusiam.

"Good news?" a weak but suddenly hopeful patient responds.

"Yes, a new medication called Verostin has just been approved by the Food and Drug Administration that has proven to cure your condition within an average of 5 days!"

"Doctor, you've got to be kidding me! How can I get this new medication?"

"Well, just let me examine your condition one last time, and I think that we can get a hold of it by tomorrow morning."

All night long Mr. Rentería feels for the first time in a long time the peace and the joy of knowing that at last a cure has been found. He finally drifts off to sleep, and surprisingly with even much less pain than before.

The sun light of the morning moved through Mr. Rentería's window waking him to the delight and anticipation of his newly found cure.

The door opens to his room. "Good morning, Mr. Rentería, I have the Verostin that you have been waiting for." The doctor takes out of the top left pocket of his white lab coat a small plastic cylindrical container of what looks to be about 100 purple and yellow capsules.

"Take two capsules in the morning on an empty stomach, and two again in the evening just before you retire. It may make you feel a little dizzy on the first day, but that is normal. Take you four capsules daily with the schedule that I just gave you, and you should see a big improvement within only 5 to 7 days."

"Can I take my first two capsules now? I haven't eaten anything."

"Go right ahead."

Just like the doctor predicted, Mr. Rentería felt a little dizzy on the first day. The second day, 50% of the pain and discomfort had gone. By the third, day to his delight, Mr. Rentería was pain free. By day number 5, all of his strength had returned and all of the lumps and visible tumors had disappeared. Mr. Rentería was beside himself with glee. "I can't wait to show Dr. Goldman my progress. These capsules are miraculous!"

As if by coincidence, Dr. Goldman walks in with all of the tests of the last 3 days. "Mr. Rentería, you have been shown to be the most remarkable and responsive patient with this new medication that we have had to date. I am happy to tell you that your tumors, all of them, have all dissolved and disappeared! How do you feel?"

"Oh, doctor, doctor, doctor, I feel *great!!*"

"Well, Mr. Rentería, I think that we can let you go home now, but I want to have you come in for a weekly check up for the next 6 months. Is that okay with you?"

"You bet, doc!"

The Placebo Effect

Mr. Rentería was discharged from the hospital healthy as can be and fully recovered from the cancer, but little did he know that what Dr. Goldman had given him was no more than a placebo or just sugar pills. What had really cured Mr. Rentería was his "positive expectation" or belief in the medication. This phenomenon "the placebo effect" has been seen and reported countless times since the early 60's when patients have taken medication believing that is would cure them even though what they took was no more than innocuous sugar pills. Though doctors love to label things believing that they have explained them, if we truly look at the psycho-dynamic of "the placebo effect," we see the truth that was stated in the holy scriptures of the Bible, *"According to your faith, so be it unto you."–Matthew 9:22"*. What doctors fail to see and get excited over is the incredible healing power of positive expectation. We are still talking about the power of belief here, but we are also talking about a very powerful and creative use of your mind.

What You Expect, You Get

The road to getting whatever goal it is that you wish to achieve is that you must *expect* to get it. When you expect the best, you release a powerful and magnetic force. This powerful and magnetic force becomes the Law of Attraction (which we will cover at length in a later chapter of this book). If you expect the worst to happen, the worst will somehow befall you. If you expect the best, you will be led to the ways and means of creating the best way to rapidly create whatever it is that you desire. Maintain yourself in a state of sustained expectation of the best. Positive attitude and faithful expectancy is the key.

You Can Develop Your Positive Expectation Muscle

It may come as no surprise to you that what you don't use you lose, at least

"Proscrastination is the thief of time."–Edward Young

temporarily, and what you practice strengthens. I am here to tell you the good news that you can most definitely develop, just as you would a muscle and to a very high degree, your power and ability to feel positive expectation. The key to doing this is to "talk" to yourself. You can do this anytime or anywhere, but I suggest that you select on a daily basis a special positive expectation practice location. Would you like to know where I want to suggest that that place be? The shower. When you bath, in the morning and/or at night. You will find yourself getting cleansed on the outside and on the inside. And just being in a cleaning and cleansing environment is the perfect subconscious mental metaphor. Say certain things to yourself like, *"I know that Life (God) is with me, and I know that everything will turn out fine." "I am a good-luck magnet." "I expect the best and the best is coming to me now."* Just do this everyday for just 30 days straight and no more, then write me with your results. I will be expecting good things that you will tell me.

"Chance does nothing that has not been prepared beforehand."–Alexis de Tocqueville

"You are not only who you are today but also who you choose to become tomorrow."–
Melvin Powers

The Law of Detachment

You have decided what it is that you want; you have written down your goal, and you have taken action on the plan that you have created. Now what? You at this point, have two choices, you will become patient and trusting of what happens, or you will become impatient, doubtful and become upset at whatever happens that is not exactly according to your plan. No where in the universe does there exist a perfectly straight line. All of your plans are the rough drafts of your desired life script which are *always* edited and modified by unexpected events and the surprises of Higher Power (God). Do you *really* want a script that is *totally* predictable? (Remember the plight of total predictability of Rocky Valentine in chapter 1 of this book.) Therefore we must *expect* temporary setbacks and stubbling blocks on the path to our purpose and onto whatever goals we may have set. Would you ever go to a movie that was completely predictable, had no problems, no challenges and no adventure to face? Of course not. You would say, what a boring movie script. And then you stand up and chear when the protagonist or hero of the story, gets determined, gets resolved and makes a glorious comeback. Now *that's* a great movie! What makes you think that God doesn't know how to write a good movie plot. He does it everyday with our lives. But so many of us try to outwrite God. So many of us feel that Higher Power doesn't know what it's doing. Ever heard the saying, "Let go. Let God"? Well, it's true. We must learn to trust that Unifying Force which created all and knows perfectly well how to run the universe to show us the best ways to achieve our desired goals.

"Men don't fail, they only stop trying."—Anonymous

The Magic of Present Moment Living

We must, in order to be both successful and happy, learn how to live in the present moment. This goes to the heart of what this chapter is about – detachment. Detachment means letting go of our "perfectly fixed" daily agendas. We may plan and we may have a goal, but we must be like the running brook which, though flows purposely seeking the ocean, twists and turns and moves around and over all obstacles in its path until it runs its course and enters, at long last, into the banks of the open water. Living in the present moment means being conscious of what must be done this day that will bring us closer to our goal. We must resist the worry and doubts of tomorrow. What is happening right now that you should be paying attention to? What is it that you know you must be doing right now to bring you closer to your goal? Higher Power can only speak to us and guide us from the vantage point of the now. In terms of where true reality lies, it cannot be in the past, and surely is not in the future. What is left is only the present moment. Even if our goal is to squeeze more love and joy out of life, we must learn to seize the day and know and appreciate the present moment of today.

Many years ago when I was about 21 years old, I was inspired over a course of 3 days. Ideas came to me and evolved into an essay about the importance of present moment living. I said that one day I would publish this essay for all who might appreciate its message. Now is the moment that I would like to offer it to all. I call it "Let Us Live Life Now".

Let Us Live Life Now (An Inspired Essay) by Charles Prosper

How many of us are letting life whiz by? How many of us are letting irretrievable time pass us, as we continue to look over the horizon, waiting to live for that magical wonderland which is to come? How many years will be wasted before we are enlightened and realize that our waiting-to-live is such a tragic farce?

An explosive illustration of the above can be seen in this quote by Stephan Leacock: "How strange it is, our little procession of life! The child says, 'When I am a big boy.' But what is that? The big boy says, 'When I grow up.' And then, grown up, he says, 'When I get married.' But to be married, what is that after all? The thought changes to 'When I'm able to retire.' And then, when retirement comes, he looks back over the landscape traversed; a cold wind seems to sweep over it; somehow he has missed it all, and it is gone. life, we learn too late, is in the living, in the tissue of every day and hour."

Life must be captured in its movement. Life lies in its progression, not after the fulfillment of goals, because once all goals are fufilled there is no more life.

Implicit within this concept of life is its central purpose: enjoyment. Every activity a human being engages in is goal-oriented consciously or unconsciously. Therefore, everything one does should be either potentially or immediately directed to enjoyment.

Life is like a trip on a train. We either look out the window and enjoy the colors, sights and panorama of the landscape as we pass them by,

---

"The deed is everything, the glory nothing." –Johann Wolfang von Goethe

THE LAW OF DETACHMENT

or we sleep throughout the entire ride, only to awaken at the end of our road. Is it that the trip is as important as the reaching of the destination?

Life is like an exquisite and sumptuously prepared banquet placed before us. The individual who races through the appetizers and entrée, to be able to quickly get to and finish with the dessert, has overlooked that the pleasure of the banquet, and life, is in the savoring of it, bite by bite, each and every part of it. We cannot listen to a completed piece of music – all at once; we can only enjoy it as it moves through us – note by note. Fulfillment should not be exalted to the near exclusion of the progression. Progression and fulfillment should be considered as one on an ever intensifying continuum, that is, fulfillment is progression, at its highest and most glorious stage.

We should try to approach life as a never-ending progression of enjoyment. We should think more of the _now_ movement. We should begin to _live_ more within the _now_ movement. Since the progression or movement toward a goal is usually longer than the experience of its fulfillment, then one should be aware of and try to experience the joy of the progression as _well_ as the fulfillment.

"In basketball and in life, you'll always miss 100% of the shots that you don't take." –Charles Prosper

An important concept to the understanding of enjoying the progression of life lies within the concept of stimulus variation, or simply "experience". In 1954, a group of scientists, by the names of Benton, Heron and Scott, did an experiment at McGill University where college students were paid $20.00 a day (a lot of money in 1954) to do absolutely nothing.

For 24 hours a day, they laid on comfortable beds in a room kept at an even temperature. Their eyes, ears and hands were shielded to minimize stimulus variation. Whereas some individuals chronically complaining of the drugery of having to get up and go to work every morning would consider this situation a utopian means of making a living. The fact was that under the conditions of the experiment, few subjects could endure more than 2 or 3 days! The craving for stimulus variation was overwhelming!

Stimulus variation is anything that can be experienced. It could be eating an ice cream cone, being depressed through a love lost, attending a church revival, or meditating on life. Stimulus variation means experience. Experience is the synonym for life, for living _implies_ experiencing. Life should be a continuum of achieving higher and higher levels of experience. Variety is indeed the spice of life, and stimulus variation _is_ necessary for the emotional satisfaction and happiness of the human organism. Inertia is anathema. One _is_ happiest when he is vitally absorbed in something which interests him. Even pain can deepen and mature, sometimes opening consciousness to a more profound understanding of life.

I often thought that a world <u>completely</u> without any problems or needs would be utopia, but now I wonder. If there are no problems or needs, there can be no goals. If there are no goals, there is no life, activity or stimulus variation toward its fulfillment. If there is no stimulus variation, as was noted above, there will be no emotional satisfaction, therefore no enjoyment, therefore no happiness. Is then suffering, pain and problems a reflection of the infinite intelligence and benevolence of the universe?

Since absorption and activity are so vital to the emotional well-being of the individual, we are naturally led into what forms the core of all our activity: our daily work. Alas, far too many people find their daily "work" and unenjoyable and unpleasant experience. As I once read: "Nothing is really work, unless you would rather be doing something else."

Too many jobs are ill-chosen on the basis of the salary alone. Sorry is the man or woman who lives only from payday to payday at a job which he or she despises. The <u>majority</u> of our lives are spent on the jobs or in the careers we have chosen. Can we really afford such a waste? For all we know the life we have may end tomorrow.

"It wasn't raining when Noah built the ark."–Howard Ruff

I find that sadly too many of us live sporadically and in pieces by finding life only when we "go out and have a ball" instead of also living, enjoying and experiencing life – <u>right</u> <u>now</u>.

A happy gardener who enjoys the jokes, laughter and conversation of his co-workers, the beauty of the landscape and has the appreciation in his heart of being able to express his joy through his work is much more "successful" in life than the pressured executive who has gone for the third time for the treatment of his stress-induced ulcers.

So let us stop putting off the living and loving of life, for living and loving and enjoying life can only be in the present moment. Let us capture it. Let us awake from our stupor. Let us at last silence the echoing laughter of the tyrant Time, who devours our lives as we endlessly wait for him to bring us into an impossible experience of the receding future.

Whew! I finally got that out of my system. I had had this essay sitting in my closet of papers for over 37 years. Finally, I have been able to give these thoughts to the world. I feel like a fruit laden tree that was just able to lighten a load of fruit that had been pulling down and hanging from its branches for years. I hope you enjoyed it and were able to apprectiate the message.

What Does Detachment Mean?

In essence, detachment means, you do your thing, and let God do His thing. Your job is to chose what you want, intend to have it, take action, and know that what you want will happen if you just stay positive and don't overly worry about the details of the "how" of that which will happen much further down the line where you have no idea of what challenges you will need to face. At this point, you must learn to detach from a specific result. Whatever happens after you have done your part may manifest as some form of problem you may have to solve, that is, your next stepping stone. Even when you are climbing a straight stairway to the top, you may tire. Each step, after so many, becomes an effort, even if you know where it will end. Your job is to keep stepping up your spiral staircase, even though the top pearces through the clouds before you are able to see it. Detach from the need to see everything visible all at once. The higher you climb, the more you will see.

You ability to detach lies in your ability to have faith in something much greater than yourself. You have boarded the plane. You just can't fly the plane. God is the pilot. You are the passenger. As long as you have paid for your ticket, through diligent planning and decisive action, you may get on board and find your seat. But when you hit an air pocket of turbulence, and the plane starts to shake a little, you still must *trust the pilot*. If you don't trust the pilot, why in heavens did you get on board in the first place?

"Scoundrels are always sociable." –Arthur Schopenhauer

Detachment is Acceptance, and Acceptance is Peace

In essence, detachment means, you do your thing, and let God do His thing. Your job is to chose what you want, intend to have it, take the risks, and observe the results. If something works, do more of it. If something does not work, notice that too, and do less of it. You see, this take-action observation-of-results, and the changing-of-your-approach is your "dialogue" between you and Higher Power. If you are caught up in worry or lamenting why something did not turn up as exactly as planned, you became attached to a specific result instead of enjoying the experience of your personal and spiritual evolution. This is the way of character building when you face a disappointment, detach and start all over again–with a refined and more enlightened approach.

Even when what you desire is more peace, happiness and better relationships with your friends, family and co-workers, the importance of detachment is at the core of this achievement of perfect and balanced interpersonal human relationships as well. In fact, generally speaking, the key reason for failure in most human relationships is the psychodyamic of making it important that persons behave in certain prescribed ways that we have deemed to be the best way for them to behave, and that they should react to their environment exactly as we would.

Detachment is the Key to Happiness and Success

Detachment is a concept that has been embraced more in Eastern philosophy than in the West. The underlying principle, as previously mentioned of detachment, is acceptance – acceptance that we are living in a perfect, balanced and just universe, based on laws of cause and effect. That we may not always know the ultimate cause of everything is a given, and that we are often times in a squabble that things aren't as we would like them to be, is the primary foundation for stress. When it comes to happiness and success, the principle of detachment is simple: if there is something that you think is wrong that you can change or improve – just improve or change it! If you can't change or improve it, for now, just accept it. This is what happiness, success and detachment is all about. Those who detach and accept operate under the premise that the universe has been here, and running efficiently, before we happened to arrive. Whatever Intelligence has created continues to know exactly what events ought to happen and when. This freedom from worry (this peace of mind), comes from a trust (belief) in something greater than one's human self who knows <u>exactly</u> what to do. There is even a famous prayer of detachment know in the western world as the Serenity Prayer that goes like this:

> God grant me
> the courage
> to change the things that I can,
> the serenity
> to accept the things that I can't
> and
> the wisdom
> to know the difference.

Detachment and acceptance walk happily hand-in-hand. You cannot have one without the other. Another component of detachment is patience and non-judgement. Patience and non-judgement look at a situation or person that is behaving in a way which we are not in agreement and decides to accept the person or situation just as it is. Your spouse who is quiet and soft-spoken, does not have to change just to satisfy your ego need for her to be as you think that she "should" be. If a friend is a little overweight, in your opinion, and you are an exercise enthusiast, or if you have had great recent success in business and you see a friend or relative procrastinating on starting a business that you think would be great for them, it is not necessarily a "good" idea to believe that they "should" be or do "better". That is just where they

"Do not look to God to do something that you are not willing to do for yourself."–
Charles Prosper

THE LAW OF DETACHMENT

happen to be right now on their path. Love them and let them be. Help when asked. Avoid trying to design other people lives. It is God's job to inspire, not yours. If you think that people should be, do and have something that *you* think is best for them before they are ready, willing or inspired to do so, you tacitly trying to occupy the place of a deity. This is not your place. Don't <u>*should*</u> on the people you love.

One last thing before we get off the subject of detachment, those who are without attachments cannot be manipulated for it is only through an a attachment to an idea that a particular thing *must* happen that you can be controlled. Detach from the fear of losing that which another dangles before you, and allow for that thing to disappear as would an imaginary carrot disappearing before the enlightened donkey.

On your road to happiness and success, detachment and acceptance of what is, are always the key processes that will produce your peace, calmness and good judgement. You are only as happy, serene and successful as the thoughts you habitually choose to think.

"It is easier to resist at the beginning than at the end." –Leonardo da Vinci

"You are not only who you are today but also who you choose to become tomorrow."–
Melvin Powers

CHAPTER 6

The Law of Attraction

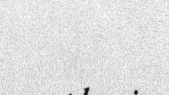

Of all of the 12 Laws of the Universe, the Law of Attraction is surely one of the most popular, and well, uh...the most attractive. In essence, the Law of Attraction states that whatever you habitually focus on, you tend to attract automatically into you life. This law is very appealing to most people because of its apparent promise of effortless manifestation of the things that they want in their lives. However, if we really want something, that means we are focusing on it, and since we are focusing on it, therefore it is being attracted into our lives. Right? Well, there is a little more to it than that. If it were as easy as that then everyone who has ever really want something would always walk away with their arms loaded down with all of the stuff they could imagine. There are also many things that can and do get in the way of the Law of Attraction. One of those things is doubt and worry. This is the killer for most people. Another thing that stops the Law of Attraction is the refusal to take immediate and positive action to make that which you say you want to come about. You see, the minute that you focus your energy on something, by the laws of Higher Power, that which you have begun to think about begins to move toward you with the intention of becoming reality. This movement toward you appears in the form of opportunity. The problem is also that many of us do not recognize this first of the manifestation of our desire because we sometimes misread the opportunity when it appears. Only in hindsight we say, "I should not have doubted myself and hesitated. I should have taken that risk, and I should have gone for it." We frequently miss our cues. If fruit falls to the ground after we have prayed for food, we *still* have to bend over and *pick* it in orde to eat it. The Law of Attraction is not the law of imposition, that is, you are never forced to realized what you have focused on and have thought about.

"If you are not leaning, no one will ever let you down." –Anonymous

Read Your Goal Card and Your Plan Twice Daily

Why do you imagine that the advice given the most by experts on goal setting and goal achieving is to read your written goals daily out loud, once in the morning and once just before retiring? This practice impregnates your subconcious mind with the energy essence of your goal. On the first level, what is sure to happen is these thoughts will attract like thoughts. Thoughts are creative, and they like to produce more of their kind. Have you noticed that when you are creatively inspired, you tend to think of more and more thoughts of the same thoughts? And conversely, when you are in a state of worry or grief, have you noticed that you tend to produce more and more thoughts of that kind? Why is this?

Isaac Newton's Law of Physics

Isaac Newton explain the Law of Attraction like this: "A body in motion tends to remain in motion until acted upon by an outside force." There is also a corollary law of physics to this law which is the Law of Accelerated Acceleration. What this means is that as objects are attracted to eachother, as they come closer and closer to each other, they accelerate in speed or velocity. If you drop a 3-inch metal ball from atop a table to the floor, and if you drop that same 3-inch ball from an airplane 30,000 feet up, the force of the velocity hitting the ground from the airplane will have an impact tens of times greater than that of the drop from atop the table. Long-range goals almost always tend to have more power and force when they appear in your life after the long and diligent years of working toward it, versus goals that you have planned to accomplish for tomorrow.

The Rich Get Richer, and The Poor Get Poorer

This is not an unfair edict. This is the result of the knowledge or the ignorance of the Law of Attraction. If you think rich, prosperous thoughts and take rich and prosperous actions, you will attract rich and prosperous results. If you think poor, miserable thoughts and take poor and miserable actions, you will attract poor and miserable results. Your thought-magnets produce unto its on kind. Is this what the Nazarene meant when he pronounced the mystic phrase, *"For whosoever has, to him shall be given, and he shall have more abundance: but whosoever has not, from him shall be taken away even that which he has"*—Matthew 13:12. That which one must have is the *consciousness of having*, that is, the belief of having and the knowing expectation of having.

There are other popular expressions that fill our lexicon with the demonstration of the awareness and observation of the Law of Attraction. "Birds of a feather flock together." "When it rains, it pours." "Tell me who are your friends, and I can tell you who you are."

The Law of Attraction is both a positive and negative force depending on the nature of the thought. Have you ever heard of a person who is "jinxed", that is, no matter what he or she does always seems to attract bad luck? Ever heard the expression that so-and-so is "accident prone"? And conversely, I am sure that you have heard once or twice the expression, "She has the luck of the Irish", not that the Irish, as

If you stick your head in the sand, one thing is for sure, you'll get your ass kicked."–Anonymous

a group are necessarily more lucky than anyone else, but rather that all of these colloquial expressions are commenting on observable patterns that can be explained by the Law of Attraction.

Thoughts Attract Like Thoughts

Through the Law of Belief, we learned that whatever is your dominate thought or whatever is the nature of your dominate belief system, so will be your experience. Thoughts have a sticky nature to them. If you start your day in a negative mode, the tendency is that it will continue to go in a downward spiral until you have become more and more negative by the end of the day, like the expression of "getting up on the wrong side of the bed" meaning that my day started out bad and has continued this way all day long. Remember Sir Isaac Newton's law of motion, "A body in motion tends to remain in motion until acted upon by an outside force." Unless you do something to act upon the directional force of a given thought pattern, it will continue ever-increasing in that direction. The point is that, left to themselves, thoughts behave like drunkened monkeys in a china shop who will open the door and let more and more drunkened monkeys inside. You must control your thoughts, by doing whatever it takes to change your negative thought patterns the moment you notice them.

"The biggest risk in life is not risking."–Anonymous

Nipping Negative Thoughts in the Bud

The total control over your negative thoughts when they arise is time-sensitive. You can only have total control over them in the beginning, when you first notice them, but it is extremely difficult if not temporarily impossible to control them when the have arisen to full force. We see this metaphor of timely control all throughout the natural world. If I take a marble and roll it down the side of a snowy mountain, assuming that this marble will collect and grow snow around it the further it rolls down the snowy slope, as it picks up momentum the marble will become a snowball the size of a baseball, then the size of a basketball, then the size of a 5 foot exercise ball. It continues to roll, now it is the size of a round 20 foot snow-covered boulder. It continues to roll. Now, it is the size of a 1 story house. It continues to roll even more. Faster. Faster. Faster! Now, it is the size of a 5 story building. "Avalanche!" the people cry out in the village. Frantic screams of terror. People scattering around in confusion, crashing into eachother, attempting to save their lives. The giant rolling snowball has now reached the size of the Empire State Builing. All is lost. The village and all of the people below are decimated.

Let's take another example to illustrate the principle of *early-stage* thought control. Unfortunately, many people still have the pernicious and nasty habit of smoking. You are on vacation in Europe, and you are seated on an outside café having a bit of espresso. The gentleman next to you, who is smoking a cigarette, stands up to go to the restroom. With red hot ashes dangling from the tip of his lit cigarette, he passes by brushing lightly against your shoulder. In that instant, by accident, a bit of the red hot ash falls on the wool pants of your right pants leg. You have two choices. You either react quickly and brush the hot ash off of your pants leg before it does any damage, or you can look at the burning ash in dismay and disbelief and allow it to burn a hole in your pants and scorc the top of your flesh. Of these two options, the saner would be to quickly flick the hot ash off of your pants before it has a chance to do any damage. In the case of the rolling marble down the snowy mountain, the sanest action would be to grab the marble before it could roll down more than a few inches. And, so it is likewise when you are tempted to become angry, upset, judgemental, frustrated or vindictive. If you can notice the marble rolling down the hill or the cigarette ash landing on your pants, in the first few seconds, you can grab that marble, or you can flick the ash off of your pants.

Let us say that someone cuts you off on the freeway, and gives you the middle finger. You now have one of two options: You can smile and wish that person well, or you can do nothing and allow the insult to fester and within minutes allow the snowball to get out of control where you are cursing and swearing, and in a foaming fit of rage – which then can continue all day as you remember and replay the incident in your mind. I am not saying that this type of self-control is easy, I am only saying that it is *necessary* for you happiness and peace of mind. Your spouse unfairly criticizes you, or your boss reprimands you for something that was totally unavoidable. Here again you have one of two choices: You can forgive and forget, or you can fume and fret. This whole thing of forgiveness, I know, is not easy. It is a new habit that has to be formed. Some will have a harder time at forming the "quick-forgive" habit than others; some people have taught themselves to become addicted to impatience and to be in judgement of others. But if your goal is more peace and joy, I can show you an easy technique out of this reactionary abyss. The second that you notice that you are about to react negatively to something, say to yourself (out loud if the situation permits, but at least subaudibly to yourself with emotion and feeling) *"I love life and I love peace of mind more than any situation!"* Repeat this at least 10 times until you feel the initial temptation to react subside. I actually recommend, as we say in bodybuilding parlance, do 3 sets of 10 reps. This means that you repeat, *"I love life, and I love peace of mind more than any situation!"* out loud if possible 10 times. Rest for one minute, then repeat is again for another 10 reps (or repetitions). Rest for another minute, then repeat it again for your 3rd set of 10 reps. By now, you should easily have interrupted the pattern

"Others can stop you temporarily, but only you can do it permanently." –Anonymous

and have created a "homeostasis" or emotional balance for yourself once more. Positive thinking leads to more positive thinking. Positive thinking leads to positive feeling. Positive feeling will always lead to positive action, and positive action will always lead to positive experience. Isn't this what really want?

Notice How You Are Feeling, For This Is What You Attract

The most accurate barometer to know what you are attracting into your life right now is to notice how you are feeling. Good feelings are attracting good experiences, and bad feelings are attracting bad experiences. All of us know without any instruction from a book what a good or a bad feeling is like. We have placed different labels on either good or bad experiences which may help us categorize somewhat the nuances of what's going on, but like all labels to explain the "invisible," they will always be less than perfect. Good experiences fall within the broad labels of peace, love and joy. Bad experiences fall within the broad labels of anger, fear and sadness. If you can keep yourself in a state of positive forgiving, loving and peaceful feelings, just 80% of the time, I can promise you a healthy, happy and successful life.

Love and Fear Are the Two Major Opposing Forces

Most people believe that the opposite of love is hate. Not so. The opposite of love is fear. Either your feelings are a facet of fear or a facet of love. Hate is the *response* of fear because hate results when one feels threatened, overwhelmed and out of control because of something or someone. The innate response to fear and the perceived "threat-of-overwhelm" is to destroy or eliminate that which is causing these uncomfortable and debilitating feelings. In a weird, strange twist of the mind, one begins to feel that resentment and hatred is the way to "get back" at that person or thing. It really isn't. It doesn't result in even a fraction of the harm that it does to you first. I will give you a tip for keeping the upper hand on the temptation to fall into the traps of any fear. Love and bless your challenge, and ask how might you learn from it, in order to grow and to become more peaceful. Let me put this in the first person and demonstrate an alternative reaction to the stress of daily life. The next time something happens to you that you *think* should not have happened to you, try this for the next 30 days whenever you feel disappointed. Just say to yourself, preferably out loud for 3 sets of 10 reps, *"I love and I bless this situation, even though in this moment I do not understand why, and I ask what is it that I might learn from it to grow and become a more peaceful and loving person?"* Try this each time you are tempted to become upset, just for the next 30 days, then write me and tell me if I am spot on with this advice.

"What we Are is God's gift to us. What we Become is our gift to God."–Robert Anthony

"You are not only who you are today but also who you choose to become tomorrow."–
Melvin Powers

CHAPTER 7

"Success is when you do what you say you're going to do." –Emily Ruth Goins (author's mother)

The Law of Planning

You start with your goal, but and follow up with a plan. A plan focuses the energy of your intention. When you plan to do something that is just in your mind, it has a tendency to dissipate from your consciousness and appear distant and dreamlike. When you write your goal down and when you write down your well-thought out and detailed plans to carry out your goal, you give your goal its first physical reality even if, at the moment, it is only on paper. However, keep in mind that plans are not fixed and unflexible entities. A plan is a dynamic organism; it lives, breathes and expands. It evolves as you do. It grows and changes as you do. The idea is to start where you are with what you have and with what you know that ought to be done. As you begin to execute your plan, you will begin to see what else needs to be done or what needs to be modified, changed or eliminated, and thus you change your approach and you re-adapt your plans.

You see, God wants to play in your game too. You serve with an overhand shot, and God volleys back with a backhand that will force you in another direction allowing you to see something that you might have not seen had you not looked the other direction the ball was hit. And the strange yet wonderful thing about this Divine Tennis Partner is that He is playing in a way to make *sure* that you win! When my daughter, Luzemily, was eight-years old she loved to play checkers with me. If I beat her several times in a row, she would get frustrated and wouldn't want to play with me anymore. So, I changed my checker-playing strategy. *Somehow,* everytime we'd play, she would be me five out of five times and ten out of ten times. She was so happy, and her sweet little eyes lit up so brightly.

"Ah, ha, ha, ha! I beat you again, daddy!"

"You most certainly did, baby girl. How did you *do* that?"

I think God plays like this with us as well.

The Two Major Aspects of The Law of Planning

There are two major aspects of the Law of Planning which are:

1. Making Plans

2. Protecting Plans.

I want you to think about this a second. After you decide upon a goal and begin to create and write down your plans, what is it that the majority of people do? They begin to talk to others, family, friends, or co-workers about what they are going to do. Then what comes next is even more dangerous – asking people for opinions! Yes, I did say the word dangerous because this practice can spell the immediate end and the death of your dream.

Don't Ask for Opinions (From Friend and Family)

Right now, we are on the subject of achieving an important life goal that you have chosen, be it a new career or a new business. If you are that type of person who will typically ask for opinions from others before you undertake any new and inspired idea, I can uneqivocally say to you that you have, to this day, <u>not</u> acheived any of your important goals because of this very pernicious habit. The confusion lies in not understanding the difference between an <u>opinion</u> and a <u>fact</u>.

Opinions are just that opinions. They are not facts. There is a <u>big</u> difference between an opinion and a fact. A fact is after the action takes place. What I am trying to say is that in the asking of an opinion (which is motivated mostly by <u>fear</u>) you are attempting to predict the future via somebody else's idea about the thing. When you really think about it, when well-intentioned, misguided and misinformed advice is given, you <u>yourself</u> will <u>still</u> have to go our and prove or disprove it by *doing!* The problem with opinions is that it shifts the center of power from where it should be – *inside of yourself*, to where it should not be – *outside of yourself*. The other problem with opinions is that 99% of them are oftentimes laced with the cyanide of negativity. "You can't do *that!*" "I have a cousin who tried something like that, and he went bankrupt!" are very common reactions.

Now let me make something perfectly clear. There is a vast difference between these two things:

- getting an opinion

- gathering <u>information</u> from experts.

But be careful that even when you ask information from experts that it does not become a cleverly disguised opportunity for *getting an opinion.* Let me explain. You go to an expert on building wooden shelves, and ask him how to build shelves which would be able to hold heavy boxes in a storeroom. This would be *gathering information.* To ask that same expert on shelve building whether you should open the business for which these shelves are intended, would be *asking for an opinion.* When you ask for an opinion, you are essentially asking some-

"You will always find time for that which you love to do-no matter how 'busy' you are." –Charles Prosper

one *else* for permission to believe in yourself. No one can *ever* do this for you. To believe in *your* idea, *your* dream or *your* vision is a very personal thing which comes to you from God to you, and must be carried to fruition because of *your* faith, not that of another.

I like the way the U.S. military does it. When they have a plan that is part of a special mission, all information is classified on a *"need to know"* basis. There may be thousands of people working on a project each with different skills and different types of expertise, yet they are allowed to know only so much to get the particular job that they are assigned to do. Many times the engineer that is contracted to create a certain type of propeller doesn't know if it is for a rocket ship to Mars or the propulsion engine that will launch a new atomic missile. I like the way the Nazarene put it, *"Do not let the right hand know what the left hand is doing."*–Matthew 6:03

Now here's a biggie. What I will say next may shake the foundation of one of the most important life decisions you have made. You may need to time at what stage you think it would be best to reveal your dream to your spouse. Sometimes, you can tell them up front. Sometimes it may be necessary for you to begin until you have it sufficiently underway that he or she will see and be convinced of your seriousness. However, if you cannot share your most heartfelt dream with a spouse without him or her scoffing, doubting or ridicuing you, it may be time for you to seriously think about unhooking the caboose.

The main problem with asking for opinions is *when the person gives you a negative opinion? Now,* what do you do? Now, you must compelled to *defend* your idea. Whatever you must defend, weakens you. Family and friends will sometimes give you negative opinions because they are coming from no knowledge, experience, or faith in what you are trying to do. Your vision is a precious and sacred gift. Keep your visions to yourself. Be willing to do whatever is necessary, but do that which must be done silently. You can show your idea to the whole later where it will be a *fact* and not an opinion.

Don't Tell People What You Are Going to Do

The sister of *asking for opinions* is *telling people what you are going to do*. Why would you tell anybody what you're going to do if it were not for your need of approval which is the same thing as the *need for a positive opinion*. The problem is, when you go out sharing your plans and dreams with everybody who will listen to you, you are in essence unwittingly *expecting* a *positive* opinion from everybody. Even if several people in a row tell you, "That's great! I think that's a great idea!", there is still a danger there. You may become addicted to hearing praise of people so that whenever you have a doubt, a new idea or an innovative plan, you will go back to these people looking for second and third

"The best way to escape from any problem is to solve it."–Anonymous

helpings of praise. Eventually, someone is going to disagree with an idea that you believe in. And whether you understand it or not, many, many people interpret your telling them of what you are going to do as an *invitation* for them to give you their opinions. Since you have placed other people in charge of your motivation, the worst can happen. You may discard a good idea in favor of a friend's opinion.

Talking-about-it becomes a substitute for doing. Talking-about-it gives your mind the illusion that you have actually done something. You talk all of your spiritual energy out of yourself. You need to conserve your visions within. You need to operate like the old-fashion steam engine which used its steam to move itself forward instead of just *blowing off steam*.

You Are the Pregnant Mother of Your Dream

In a metaphysical and spiritual sense, when you are inspired by an idea from God, you have been fertilized with the seed of the Universe to carry out a certain mission. God is the father. You are the mother. Your dream is the child to be born. What is the purpose of motherhood? The sole purpose of motherhood is to protect the unborn child. This is immediately and obviously evident by the fact that the unborn child is covered and hidden from the world inside of the mother. After the development is complete, after nine long months, the child may be born and shown to the world. What if the imprudent mother in her excitement and pride tries to show her baby to the world too soon and decides to have an early Cesarean birth after a couple of months because she just can't wait. The result would be obvious. The baby would not be able to survive exposed too soon to the outside world. This is exactly what happens to your dream-child when you decide to open up yourself to the outside before it's time. In due time, when your work is done and your job complete, you may pull back the curtains to show the world your creation. Your plans are your sacred dreams, and your silence is golden. Until your dream is ready to be revealed, everyone must be placed on *a need to know* basis.

The 7 Secret Steps to Planning

Lets' get practical. Their are 7 simple steps to planning which I would like to give to you now:

Get a legal notepad, number from 1 to 20 and write down as fast as you can twenty things that you know that you can and should do right now to make your dream a reality.

2. Create a Written Plan: Write down a series of

"It is not how much you have but how much you enjoy that creates happiness."–
Anonymous

THE LAW OF PLANNING

of steps of what you should do in chronological order. You will have two columns headings written across the top of a page: Thing To Do, on the left side and also at the top on the right side the column heading, Date Done. You may number the the planned tasks from top to bottom 1. 2. 3. 4., etc.

Notice what works, and do more of that. Notice what doesn't work, and do less of it, or eliminate it entirely.

4. Be Willing to Do Whatever It Takes: This is actu- one of the 12 Laws of the Universe which we will cover at length in a later chapter of this book. You must be willing to do whatever is necessary. The Universe will grant you anything that you are committed to.

God answers commitment with creative ideas. As you do your plan, and meet with obstacles to overcome them you will find that God will meet you midway with ideas to inspire your further. You will have more and more the "Aha!" experience.

"To know which direction to take next, you must first accept where you now are."–Anonymous

6. Act Immediately on Your New Inspirations: This is another great law. This is the Law of Immediate Action, also covered in a later chapter. Simply stated, you can't procrastinate on inspired ideas. Higher Power does not favor the procrastinator. You will notice that if you procrastinate and put off taking action on inspired, money-making ideas is that they tend to come to you less and less frequently, until they stop coming to you at all. Take immediate action on inspired ideas, or God may decide to give ideas to someone else who will take action on them. Don't be left saying, when you see some else using your origina idea, "Why didn't I just take action?"

You will soon become a very creative thinker. Incredible once-in-a-lifetime ideas will begin to pop into your head 24 hours a day. Write them down as soon as they come!

"You are not only who you are today but also who you choose to become tomorrow."–
Melvin Powers

CHAPTER 8

The Law of Willingness To Do Whatever It Takes

There is another law called the Law of Immediate Action which on the surface may appear to be the same as the Law of Willingness to Do Whatever It Takes. Similar and correlative, but they are not the same. Another way of stating this could be the Law of Willingness to Do Whatever is Necessary. Part of the implication of this law is that we always know what to do *initially*. And this is true. You may not have the *complete* or *ultimate* plan nor have all of the answers to solving a problem, but you always know *something* that you can do or should do to get yourself started. Let's say, for example, that your goal is to become a commercial airline pilot, and you know absolutely nothing about airplanes or flight. What would be some of the first and obvious things that you could do right now? Let's do this together right now. For example, you could:

1. Enroll in a flight school.
2. Read books on the construction of airplanes.
3. Talk to 20 professional pilots.
4. Study the history of airplane travel.
5. Join an organization of airplane pilots.
6. Take some seminars on becoming an airline pilot.
7. Make friends with other professional flight students.
8. Research information on the internet on airplane pilots.
9. Search for all the websites dedicated to airplane pilots.
10. Read biographies of great airplane pilots.

Now, keep in mind, without any personal interest in becoming an air-

"I do not want to be happy. I want to be at peace, for only once I am at peace can I truly be happy." –Charles Prosper

line pilot, we were able to do this quick list in less than five minutes. The point is that you must start somewhere – but with the most obvious. As you begin to do these initial things, a different set of tasks may then become obvious, many things which you were not suspecting, but they become things that you are willing and eager to do because becoming a commercial airline pilot is your dream and your passion, and you have made up your mind that nothing will stop and that no task is "too much" for you to do. "If others have done it, why can't you do it also?" is what you say to yourself.

Action Leads to More Action

The more you do. The more you are led to do. This is the law of attraction to more action. Action is thought made solid. Action attracts like action, when the action is purposeful, consistent and fueled with focus, intention, and expectancy. When I say that action attracts action I mean that your first intention to create or to do something is the catalyst that is immediately connect to a series of unseen events with infinite combinations and permutations, that all lead you to your desired goal. This is a way of saying that the more action you take, the luckier you get. Luck is when preparedness meets opportunity. If you do not have a goal or if you do not know exactly what you want and do not have the intention and willingness to act, you will neither recognize the answer to your prayers, when it appears as a "problem" or opportunity, nor will you have the ability to act on it because you had never made a decision to do so.

"Worry is a mild form of momentary atheism."–
Charles Prosper

Action Creates New Feelings, and New Feelings Create New Actions

This is the law of attraction again. As you change your beliefs, you change your experience which is what we learned in the chapter on the Law of Belief. But how do you change a belief. There are basically two major paradigms to belief-changing. You either *feel-act-believe* or you *act-feel-believe*. Either way will work. Some eternal stimulus triggers a feeling; a lover deceives you. You *feel* bad. You *act* sad. You *believe* that the situation is unbearable. The same situation can be *reversed* by the other paradigm of belief control. A lover deceives you, however you *act* happy and relieved by not having to deal with such a deceitful person anymore. If you act this way long enough, you will *feel* better. You now *believe* that you can bear this disappointment a move on with your life. William James, the father of modern psychology, put it this way.

"You need only in cold blood act as if the thing in question were real and it will become infallibly real by growing into such a connection with our life that it will become real. It will become so knit with habit and emotion that our interest in it will be those that characterize belief."

Your Willingness to Do Whatever It Takes Triggers Your Intuition

This is a phenomenon that I have experienced many times in my lifetime once I have committed to an important goal. I notice that two things will generally occur. I will receive more intuitive hunches, and more meaningful "coincidences" will start to happen. What is intuition? Intuition is that inner voice of "knowingness." It is when people say, "I have a gut feeling about (this or that)." We are born with this innate servo-mechanism. I call it the voice-of-God within. The fascinating thing about these intuitive whispers is that they happen all day – and also all night (in the form of metaphorical dream messages). The question is not whether or when God speaks to us, but rather who listens? When you trust yourself, it is another way of saying that you trust your Higher Self or the God-within. The more you trust these intuitive whispers, the more they tend to happen. Your intuition is always right. Your logical, left-brain, sceptical and doubting part of you has a sort of jealousy of the intutive mind. It is the skeptic part in you that says, "No, it couldn't be that simple." Then later you will say to yourself, "Darn! I should have followed my first mind!"

"How often does a coincidence have to happen before God is given the credit?"– Charles Prosper

Your Willingness to Do Whatever It Takes Triggers Dream Intuition

Everyone dreams, but so too many people take their dreams for granted as meaningless discharges which result from the events of the day. After having seriously studied and recorded my dreams for over 42 years, I know from first-hand experience that dreams, when interpreted properly contain, the answers and solutions to most of your daytime problems. You can even program a dream answer to any problem that you might be having, and your intuition will come through to you in the language of dream metaphors. On December 6, 2006, I awoke from a dream. I received a brilliant solution to a money-crisis that, before the dream, I had thought was impossible to solve. I quickly put the dream solution into action, and I easily solved my problem. You too can learn to program dream solutions and even program to have what's called fully-awake dreams or lucid dreams where you *know* that you are dreaming *while* you are dreaming. Intuition loves to speak to you through dreams. Once you learn how to remember them, record them and interpret them, a whole new world opens up for you. In a later chapter in this book, I will go into great detail on the incredible techniques that I have discovered for the experience of creative dreaming.

Your Willingness to Do Whatever It Takes Triggers "Coincidences"

What has fascinated me for years is the subject or the phenomena of coincidences. A meaningful coincidence occurs when an improbable event follows a prior event which is significantly related to the first. For example, you are asking yourself how can you find the answers that you seek to a particular problem, then you look up and see a freeway sign that says "Go Within." You are researching on how to buy your first home when later that evening, a friend of yours introduces you to a realtor who specializes in helping first home buyers. You are thinking about calling your sister with whom you have not spoken to in two years when at that very moment, the phone rings, and who do you think is on the other line? Your sister! Is it a coincidence, or just a chance random occurrence? It's both because God is in charge of "randomness" as He is in control of everything else that we can't seem to understand. Every coincidence happens for a reason, and that reason is that God is trying to communicate a message to us.

Just as dreams are your personal metaphors of your sleeping life, coincidences are your personal metaphors of your waking life. Coincidence is the divine language of God. How else could He get our attention if the occurrence were just ordinary and without meaning or connection to what is happening to you right now. We as humans speak one of many languages: Chinese, Russian, English, Spanish, French, Burmese, Japanese, etc. God speaks "coincid*ese*"! I often ask myself, "How often does a coincidence have to happen before God is given the credit?"

"People don't change–they camouflage."–Charles Prosper

Inspiration Unused is Merely Entertainment

When your intuitive mind gives you an inspiration, a thought or a creative idea with which to solve a problem, or to improve a situation, you must *act* upon it immediately, or you will find that inspiration will tend to come to you less and less. Maybe it does not come back less and less; maybe you only are able to hear it less and less. This immediate action is touching upon one of the other 12 great laws of the Universe which is the Law of Immediate Action. Actually all of the 12 great laws overlap and intertwine and sometimes merge all as one, but because of our limited perceptions, by choice, we fail to see their interconnectedness.

What Happens When You Are Not Willing

Whenever you know what you must do, and are not willing to immediately go into action and do whatever is necessary for the accomplishment of the goal, everything stops moving forward and temporarily shuts down! What I mean is that creative ideas slows down almost to a halt. Intuition becomes harder to hear. Fear, doubt and procrastination set in and jam up all of your forward progress. To decide not to be willing to do whatever it takes becomes a clear communication to the

Universe that you are not yet ready for Its help. Now, Higher Power must sit and wait for you to decide to become serious and committed. God helps those who helps themselves. It is not until you move that God moves.

Willingness Is A Ready-to-Go-When-Instructed Mentally

It appears that many great discoveries are often made by mistakes through the process of trying and making mistakes until the key to unlock the answer is found. The bottom line is this – as long as you are willing to do whatever is necessary, gladly and joyfully, you will achieve whatever it is that you are committed to.

"If you think you're too small to make a difference, you haven't been in bed with a mosquito." –Anita Roddick

"You are not only who you are today but also who you choose to become tomorrow."–
Melvin Powers

CHAPTER 9

The Law of Immediate Action

A law that is very, very close to the Law of Willingness to Do Whatever It Takes is the Law of Immediate Action. On the surface, they almost look to be one and the same law, but they're not. You can be willing to do whatever it takes – but just not today. Maybe tomorrow. Maybe next week. Or maybet when you get back from vacation this summer. You see, being willing also means and implies that you *will* take action immediately! If you are willing to take immediate action, what difference does it make how willing you are?

The Universe Rewards Action!

The Universe rewards action with results. The Universe rewards immediate action with immediate results. There is a library that I like to visit that is about a mile from my home. Like many modern buildings, it has a pair of automatic doors that open inward. There is a pressure-sensitive device that is outside and on the ground under a hard plastic door mat in front of the entrance. It is not until you *step forward* that the door opens. The Universe works like that library door too. It is not until you *step forward* that the door to correct knowledge and experience open inward for you. Knowing that the door to your experience opens this way, you must *step forward* first, and the door will open as you move and take action steps.

The question always becomes if someone has decided upon a desired goal and what to do next is obvious, then why is it that we don't *always* take immediate *action*. There is only one answer.

Procrastination is the Monster of Failure

We procrastinate which is another word for hesitation, doubt because we are in a fear state. The fear is usually a fear of overwhelm. We fear that we will be unable to carry out that which we say we want. So we temporarily stop ourselves and give ourselves a host of excuses and rationalizations as to why we are "not yet ready," or that we "need to prepare ourselves just a little more." Success does not work that way. When we are truly committed to something to prosper we are willing to "get rich or die trying." When you are willing to do whatever it takes, you feel the fear, but do it anyway. Also, there is another problem which

"Perfectionism is a euphemism for fear, and procrastination are its fruits."–
Charles Prosper

is in how you define the word problem. I would like to suggest to you to no longer use the word fear to describe the feeling that you have when you are about to undertake something that is new or risky. I would like for you to substitute the word "excitement" for the word fear. An *inexperienced* mountain climber feels "fear", but an experienced mountain climber feels "excitment". In the body, it is the same feeling. How you react to it depends on how you choose to label it.

Anything Worth Doing Is Worth Doing Lousy

Yes, that's right. Anything worth doing is worth doing *lousy*. Just do something anything – make corrections later. It is better to do *something* imperfectly than to do nothing *perfectly*. One of the things that get in the way of taking immediate action on the part of so many people is that they convince themselves that they must be "perfectly ready" in order to start something. No matter who you are, there is no such thing as "perfectly ready". If you were perfectly ready, if there were such a thing, would mean that you have already accomplished what you want. If you have done anything perfectly, there is nothing left to do. Perfectionism, which is no more than an unconsciously clever stalling tacit, gives you the excuse that you cannot do anything, just yet, because you are not ready. Therefore, it is easy to become in a perpetual *state of preparation* which is the *faux* justification for not being able to start. Perfectionism produces the paralysis of analysis which in turn creates a state of non-action versus one of immediately of taking aciton.

The Myth of Tomorrow

When you pray for an answer, and you get it in the form of a creative idea which you must begin to carry out, God expects immediate action from you to continue to receive His support. You must get caught up in the myth of tomorrow. There is no such thing as tomorrow. Tomorrow is just an illusion. The past is just a memory. You are always left with all that you or me ever have, the only reality – the eternal now. If you put off what it is that you must do until you arrive at what you perceive to be "tomorrow", what are you left with? You are again in the "now". Put off what you want to do for another week, another month or another year, and again you will find yourself in the now. When you start to do anything and once you finish anything, you are still in the "now". I am sure that I did not have to tell you this; you could have easily figured it out on your on, but until this insidious habit is brought to the surface in the light of common sense, we will continue as though asleep under the guise that somehow, someway the experience of life will happen to us at some point in time other than the now.

"All knowing is believing. Knowing is just believing that something is certain."–
Charles Prosper

Strike While the Iron is Hot

Inspiration is time sensitive. Don't believe it? Ask yourself, how many times you have had a great idea for a business, a book, a special project only for you to put it off and find that someone else has taken "your" idea and has run with it? When is your energy and motivation the greatest when you are inspired with a great idea? Isn't it in the beginning, when you first receive it, and providing you don't go around telling everyone about it and asking for opinions, the energy and excitement from imagining all of the possibilities, builds up inside of you more and more. It is precisely at this moment were immediate action is the most productive. Why? Because action creates more action. This again is the Law of Attraction. And the more you do immediately, the faster you will discover what you will have to do next.

Learn By Doing

Though, I most definitely believe that study and research is important, but when it is time to take action, I feel you must act quickly to create the momentum to keep going in a positive direction. Another consideration is that you will need to learn new things which don't know now in order to achieve your goal. If you knew everything that you needed to know, you would probably have already achieved your goal. To master anything requires action and thus experience which then becomes your guide for further growth. There is a built-in economy of action, and that is we learn by doing. The actions that you take will either bring you closer to your goal or further away. The formula or the secret is quite simple. Whatever you do that brings you closer to your goal, do more of it. Whatever takes you farther and farther away from your goal, do no more of it. When whatever you are doing makes things become easier and easier, you are on the right track, and when whatever you are doing makes things become more and more difficult then, you are on the wrong track.

"Everything has value. If you think 'nothing' has no value, then why do people fight over parking spaces?"–
Charles Prosper

Know When To Plan & Pray and When To Move & Make It

Would you like to hear a good joke that illustrates this idea of taking immediate and timely action? Okay. Here we go:

Eleven year old, Lisa and her six year old brother, Mark, were on the way to Sunday service where they walked from home though a lovely countryside of the small town where they lived. Today was a bright, sunny day. Birds were chirping in the trees. The fragrance of sweet white honeysuckle flowers perfumed the air. But strict instructions were given from mother that they not be late and to arrive punctually before Sunday services start. If they arrived late to Sunday school – they would be grounded for the rest of the day.

"I don't see any problem in arriving to church on time," thought Lisa, "since we left out a half hour earlier than usual."

"Yeah, look at that blue and yellow butterfly, Lisa. Isn't it beautiful!"

"It surely is, brother, and look at that view of the valley from here. We can see almost the entire town below."

"Wow!" exclaimed Mark. "It's really pretty."

They got so caught up in the beauty of the countryside that time quickly whizzed by until an unplanned 45 minutes had passed.

"Lisa! What time is it?"

"Oh, my God, it's 10:45 a.m., and it will take us at least 20 minutes to get there!"

"Do you think we will be late?" asked Mark.

"Oh, I don't know," panicked Lisa. "Maybe. Let's just kneel and pray!"

"No," replied Mark, "let's just *run* and pray!"

When you encounter the unexpected, start by taking immediate and positive action. Prayer, without positive action, is called worry. Run *and* pray!

God Speaks Through Circumstances

Once you begin immediately, God begins immediately to communicate with you. God begins to speak to you through circumstances. Let me take this even a bit further. God IS circumstances. Circumstances are really of the material body of God. This makes it easier to understand the how and why of a "coincidence". Let me explain it in a different way. Let us say that you are in a nighttime dream, and let us say that you realize that you are dreaming, also called a lucid dream. (Much more on the fascinating subject of dreams in a later chapter.) In the dream, you think of an elephant, and "coincidentally" an elephant appears. You expect to find a bag of money, and *lo and behold*, a man in a white suit walks up to you from a park bench, and says that he has been instructed to give you this leather bag containing $1,000,000 cash in one-hundred dollar bills. "Wow!" you think to yourself again. "What a coincidence!"

Now, as you sit there reading this, you are thinking, "So what, Charles. Coincidences happen all of the time in dreams." I then ask you why is it so easy for you to accept this. You then say, "Because in a dream, I am the dream and everything that is produced in the dream is really me." Consider that in your daytime dream, called waking reality, you are also the "dream" and maybe everything that is produced in this waking dream is also only you. Let me take it a step further and suggest that you are essentially a part of God. We are Divine Personalities as

"If you expect to be lucky, you will be lucky." –Anonymous-

part of God's Divine Dream of Himself.

"Peace is the pleasure of the soul."–Charles Prosper

"You are not only who you are today but also who you choose to become tomorrow."–
Melvin Powers

CHAPTER 10

The Law of Persistence

The Law of Persistence is the law of facing problems. You must accept that your progress will not move in a straight line. As I have said before, science has never been able to discover nor has been able to prove the existence of a flawlessly straight line. The problem with a straight line is that is violates the first law of creation which is that no two things created can ever be alike, and that all things created are always unique. If a straight line could exist at all it would have to exist as a phenomena which would have to be duplicateable and with no variation each time it was created. This just could not exist, that is, a multiplicity of creations which always remains the same.

However, all philosophy set aside for a moment, persistence is that quality which knows that problems are a part of progress. Persistence is also that quality which is ready, willing and able to accept them not as problems but as challenges to be overcome in the same spirit as a champion athelete faces every challenge and obstacle to ultimate victory.

The Way We See the Problem <u>Is</u> the Problem

Do you see the problem as a solveable situation or as a hopeless situation? Your positive mental attitude changes the nature of all problems. Ask yourself right now, "What does the word 'problem' mean to me?" Does it mean something that you want to avoid, want to lament or want to solve? How you answer this is always based on a decision. It is a simply matter of a decision. How you decide determines your experience. If you choose to run from or avoid a problem, "problem" will come to mean for you: fear and procrastination. If you choose to lament a problem, then "problem" will come to mean worry, going around in frenetic circles and mindless motion. If you choose to stand up, chest high and courageously, face and solve a problem, then "problem" will come to mean an invigorating and exciting game of life. My question now to you is, "Which way do you *want* 'problem' to go for you?" Make your decision, then choose that perspective. All problems are just the absence of an idea. Problems are an opportunity for growth. The beautiful part of a problem and the true design of a problem is to lead of us to self-discovery. The solution to a problem changes the nature of the problem because with every new solution, *you* change

"If you really want to do something, you'll find a way; if you don't you'll find an excuse." –Anonymous

and grow as a person.

The Creed of Calvin Coolidge (On Persistence)

Calvin Coolidge was the 30th president of the United States. He was the president who coined the phrase, "The business of America is business." Calvin Coolidge was a man of such few words that he even refused to speak to people on the telephone, but when he did speak, he had something to say. This is what he had to say about **Persistence:**

> *Nothing in the world*
> *can take the place*
> *of persistence.*
>
> *Talent will not;*
> *nothing is more common*
> *than unsuccessful*
> *men with talent.*
>
> *Genius will not;*
> *unrewarded genius*
> *is almost a proverb.*
>
> *Education will not;*
> *the world is full*
> *of educated derelicts.*
>
> *Persistence and determination*
> *alone are*
> *omnipotent.*

Persistence and Faith are Synonymous

Persistence is another word for faith in yourself for if you didn't have faith why would you persists. Ultimately, I am convinced that all faith in ourselves is a perfect reflection of our faith, consciously or unconsciously, in something much greater than ourselves, yet still an integral part of ourselves. In all of the great religions of the world and in all of their sacred texts, the power of faith is at the core of their teachings. Because my upbringing has been Judeo-Christian most of my scriptural references tend to be biblical, but that does not negate my understanding that truth has filtered through many sacred writings from many religions traditions. I have learned just as much from the teachings of Buddha, Krishna, Confucious as I have from the teachings of Jesus in the New Testament of the Bible. I accept truth wherever I find it. And remember, truth and law is testable. It will work every time.

"That which we persist in doing becomes easier–not that the nature of the task has changed, but our ability has increased."–Ralph Waldo Emerson

Persistence is the Continuous Choice of Positive Action

Committment is the choice of continuous action until the event occurs. Your success at any goal or enterprise is really a matter of when you choose to quit. *Pssst.* The secret, *just between you and me,* is that we *always* get when we persist. If you say, "There have many things in my life for which I have persisted I did *not* get!" To that I would only ask, "At what point did you quit?" You see, as long as you haven't quit, *it ain't over!* It ain't over 'til the fat lady sings. Your job is to find that fat lady, tie her up, and gag her until you reach your goal! Since from where you are to where you want to be is no more than the timely crossing over a bridge of problems, the only thing standing in your way of crossing to the side of victory is your willingness to take yet *another step forward.*

Inspired Action vs. Frantic Action

We can either become smooth and sleek greyhounds racing to the finish line or we can be running like hamsters on a circular treadmill going nowhere. There are two types of action: Frantic Action and Inspired Action. The difference in the two is that one is based on fear and the other is based on joy. If you try to start a business on a shoestring (with little or no capital) because you are about to lose your job, and you are too proud to go out and temporarily seek employment, I guarantee that you will be operating frantically, no matter how much you persists. You will be trying to swim out of quicksand where the more you persists, the faster you sink until you become completely swallowed up with sand over your head.

Inspired action is when you are starting for reasons of wanting to give and improve the quality of life for other people using your talents and special abilities. The feeling here is one of peace, joy and love. When you act, you become inspired because you know you are doing the right things and for the right reasons; Higher Power steps in and places you on His wings taking you to higher and higher heights.

"We rate ability in men by what they finish, not by what they begin." –Anonymous

How Many Frogs Were Left ? (A Riddle)

I was given this riddle by one of my mentors, Joe Sabah, world-renowned authority on book promotion using radio interviews. Here it goes:

> Three frogs were sitting on a lily pad.
> One frog decided to jump.
> How many frogs were left?

Okay, mathematicians, what is your answer? Turn the page for answer.

The correct answer is 3. Remember: to jump, and are two different things. Deciding is a *thought*. Jumping is an *action*. Action is what counts! Persistence and continuous action is what leads you to the realization of your goal.

Are You a Flea, a Grasshopper, or a Goal Achiever?

Sometimes I think that animal behavior of the natural world serves as perfect metaphors and examples as to how we should and should not behave. Well, afterall, we are the superior species, right? So, I ask you, "Are you a flea, a grasshopper, or a goal achiever?" "What? Charles, have you lost your mind?" Well, it's true some of us behave like these two insects far too often when we say that we want to achieve something that is important to us.

You can test this anytime yourself. Get a live flea, or preferably a live grasshopper, because they are easier to see. Take the grasshopper, and put it inside on the bottom of an empty glass jar. Now place the lid on the top. (Don't forget to nail air holes in the lid of the jar; they do need to breathe, you know.)

Now I want you to observe something. The grasshopper does not like the idea of confinement, so it does only what's natural. Escape! Well, that's what it tries to do. It's legs are powerful enough to jump two times higher that the top of the jar. He thinks, "A piece of cake. I can make this." He readies his powerful hind-leg muscles for an easy leap out to freedom again. He leaps! *Bamb!* He hits his head on the bottom of the closed lid. "What the f...!" he thinks, "don't know what the heck that was. No problem, I'll try again–a little harder this time." *Bamb! Bamb! Bamb!* He leaps three times to have his head met again and again with a hammering reception. After doing this again and again over several minutes and hours, our grasshopper (or flea if your dog was kind enough to lend you one) begins to jump less and less, until he learns to jump just high enough <u>not</u> to hit his head on the bottom of the closed lid. You observe now that he is still jumping, but the height of the jump is always just high enough <u>not</u> to hit the lid.

Now you may take off the lid. Just take the lid off of the jar. You will now notice that even with the lid off, the grasshopper has completely given up on the idea of jumping too high that he has trapped-himself *inside of an open jar* – as though the lid was still on! You can go about your business, even leave the open jar with the grasshopper on your kitchen table – while you eat – and this grasshopper will never be able to jump higher than just below the top of the jar.

Does this describe you? Just because you have been hit up side of the head by life several times in your attempt to achieve your goal, will you become like the grasshopper who has given up jumping so that when your opportunity *does* come, as it always does sooner or later, you

"You can overcome anything if you don't bellyache."–Bernard M. Baruch

will not to be able to achieve it? Here are two appropriate quotes to close this chapter.

> *"Never stop. One always stops as soon as something is about to happen." –Peter Brook*

> *"Many of life's failures are men who did not realize. how close they were to success when they gave up."*
> *–Thomas Alva Edison*

*"**We must look for the opportunity in every difficulty, instead of being paralyzed at the thought of the difficulty in every opportunity.**"–Walter E. Cole*

"You are not only who you are today but also who you choose to become tomorrow."–
Melvin Powers

CHAPTER 11

The Laws of Money

This is a chapter that I am sure will hold the interest of a whole lot of people: The Laws of Money. We live in an infinite, multi-layered universe. We live in a universe where a mirror faces another mirror, and we get a glimpse of infinity. Life is a circle within a circle and a dream with a dream – a major law resides within a minor law that becomes the major law of the law that which follows, and so on and so forth *ad infinitum*. What I am trying to say is that The Laws of Money is comprised of a golden web of 7 interconnected laws that form a shimmering dome of light and prosperity hovering over the person who would understand and follow them.

The First Law of Money is the Law of Saving Money

Unfortunately in our modern-day metropolitan society, we are programmed by the television, radio and magazines that to be happy we need to be spend-happy – that it is through the acquisition of "things" and more "stuff" that we can be satisfied as human beings. Just to the contrary is true. The more "stuff" we acquire, the more "stuff" we want because our essence and self-worth is based on how much we have versus how much we enjoy. If we buy into this logic, then to be more is to have more stuff. But the minute that we buy the new toy: the Jaguar, the Rolex, the high definition T.V., we, within a very short period of time *"become used to it,"* and thus set ourselves on the path to get newer and more exciting stuff. There is nothing wrong with having material possessions *as long as they don't have you*. This problem of the "malady of more" is compounded by the fact that we are programmed by the media of Madison Avenue to buy things immediately and on credit – whether we can afford to purchase it or not. Credit cards. Plastic. Nothing down. Easy monthly payments. Just pay the minimum each month. These are the traps leading to later years of scarcity and lack. It is important not to waste your prime wage-earning years squandering instead of saving your money. Though it may seem like a long time away now when you are young, time has a way of creeping up on us so that before we know it 10, 20, or 30 years have passed, and we are no closer to our dream of financial independence than when we started.

The first law of money is The Law of Saving Money because

"The best place too succeed is where you are with what you have." –Charles M. Schwab

money, and bad debt attract more bad debt.

The first law of money is the Law of Savings because money attracts money. and the purpose of money is to give you a sense of freedom from worry and stress in life. The ultimate goal of all life, whether we realize it or not, is to be at peace with life. Peace is said to be one of the three qualities to the experience of God. Peace. Joy. Love. When we have peace as a feeling-experience in our bodies, we experience the presence of God within. Peace is what we seek. Underlying the pursuit of our acquisition of material things, perfect relationships, prestige, importance, or power, the experience of any one of the feeling qualities of peace, joy or love is what we really seek. This is what we have always sought consciously or unconsciously. In modern life, in the world of complexity and interdependence of one human being on another, we seek the ultimate experience of peace, security or safety - through money. To have money, we must learn to save money. Much more on saving money a little later in the chapter.

The Second Law of Money is the Law of Control of Money

This law of control is but a subtle gradation of the Law of Saving. This is a law of understanding that you cannot have money unless your learn to control it. If you cannot control money, you will never have money. Not controlling money can take on many forms. You do not control money when you buy on credit and spend more than you have saved. You do not control money when you play the lottery with the same money that you could use to save in a long term investment retirement account (IRA) that pays you 10% per annum (per year) compounded interest which, when planned and properly executed could allow you to retire a wealthy. (More on this later.) You do not control your money when you gamble away all of your savings in casinos like those that you find in Las Vegas, Nevada. The odds of your winning a million-dollar jackpot is as good as your being able to guess the license plate of the next car that passes you by in the street. Also, let me give you a little more news about this. Even if you *did* win the lottery or the jackpot in Las Vegas, studies have shown that 99% of all lottery winners or Las Vegas jackpot winners, overspend, overgamble, give it away to undeserving relatives and friends, overpurchase expensive homes, cars, take vacation trips around the world, and other things in such excess that usually within a few years after having won this sudden money, they have returned back to their former broke state with little or no money and struggling once more. Unless you have learn to control money, even winning large somes of money will not solve your problem. You will tend to return back to whatever money comfort-zone that you had before. If you believe that if you had "enough" money that you would never have to worry about problems again, then how is it that, Mike

"Before everything else, getting ready is the secret of success."–Henery Ford

Tyson, the former world heavyweight boxing champion of the world, known for his brutal force in the quadrilateral against his opponents, knocking them sometimes high out of the ring with his devastating uppercuts, and to any whom he was not able to knock to the canvass would he summarily proceed to bite his ear off in a cannibalistic attempt at ulitmate domination – how is it that Tyson who earned a reported $900,000,000 – almost a billion dollars – in his fighting career, goes into retirement and *files for bankruptcy*? If you cannot learn to control money, it will not matter if you are given a billion dollars, you will lose it!

The Law of Money is about the control of money. You must learn to control what little you have before you are able to handle more than you have. Do you know of anyone who's gotten a raise recently? Let's say within the last year or so. Do you think that that person's savings increased by the exact amount of their raise? No. In most cases, 99% out of a 100%, that person learned to raise his or her *spending* to match the amount of the raise. If you are old enough, think back 10 or 20 years ago when you were making much less than you are earning today. Remember when you thought, "Once I am able to earn $ X amount of dollars per year, I will be on easy street!" If you are like most of us, you have probably achieved the high earnings that you formerly dreamed about. Has your financial condition changed that much? In far too many cases the answer is no. Why? Because no one ever taught us that money is not for justspending and that it is also for obtaining a sense of freedom from worry and from insecurity. We would be better served by spending our money for those things that we have saved.

"If you are seeking creative ideas, go out walking. Angels whisper to a man when he goes for a walk"–Raymond Inmon

The "Rich" Pauper

The rich pauper is a true an oxymoron! I learned of a man, in his mid-fifties, who if you looked at him on the surface, looked *super* rich. He drove a brand new factory-fresh Porsche. He wore a dazzling gold Rolex watch. He was living in a million-dollar house. So far, so good. Right? Now for the truth. Getting pass all of the trappings and accoutrements of wealth, the real story of this gentleman was that he was not only *not* rich but he was practically broke and constantly on the brink of financially failure and poverty. In that million dollar home in which he lived, he owed an $800,000 mortgage debt! He had less than $100,000 in savings, on top of which he owed more than $75,000 in credit card debt which was impossible to pay out because of the credit cards' compounding interest. When we pay the minimum payment every month, this is what the credit card companies *want* us to do. This person didn't even *own* the Porsche – he was *leasing* it! But wait – there's more. He was also paying very heavy alimony paymen to *two* ex-wives! With his earning and spending habits, his lack of control over his money, his plight was no less than the fate of Mike Tyson who let close to a *billion* dollars to pass through his fingers and then wind up filing for bankrupcty.

Americans Are Afraid to Save – We Equate Saving with Lack

Somewhere in our thinking is a bizarre core belief that saving our money is equivalent to not having money or depriving ourselves of not having enough money. If this was not the case then how do we explain these facts, according to The American Savings Education Council (Their website is **www.choosetosave.org/asec/**):

- 50% of all American workers have less than $25,000 in savings.

- 60,000,000 Americans, which is a staggering 1 in 5, have *nothing* in the bank! (How is this possible living in the richest land on earth where the average worker in America makes more than 10 times the average worker in a typical third world country!)

- The average American owes about $8,400 in credit card debt.

- 70,000,000 million baby boomers, those born between the late 1940's through the early1960's, will be reaching retirement age over the next 7 years. The American Association for Retired Persons (website **www.aarp.org/**) made a study showing that the typical baby boomer only has about $1000 worth of financial assets outside of his or her home, and this is if they happen to even own their own home; many do not.

"Never complain how heavy your groceries are."–Charles Prosper

Why is this? The reason is that we, as a society, have been taught instant gratification. We have been taught to be afraid of saving in favor of spending because saving does not satisfy our programmed and *perceived* "need" to be gratified instantly.

    My mentor, Melvin Powers, muli-millionaire mail order book publisher (website **www.mpowers.com**), once said to me years ago that as early as 15 years old he learn the magic of savings. In fact his words to me were, "Charles, it is not how much you earn, it is how much you save that matters. I have always learned to save a large porof all of my money, and I have taught myself to live off of less. My savings have compounded over the years as my income has grown. The more I made, the more I have saved. I have never borrowed a dime in my life to purchase anything. All of the houses that I have bought, I have always paid cash for them. If I want to purchase a car, I always pay cash. If I have not saved the cash for it, I simply will wait, and then I will purchase it. I have learned to live below my means to be able to save more. I have been doing this all of my business life, and I have been in business for well over 50 years. Stay away from credit card debt because the way they have set it up, you will never pay them off. Save up for what you want, and buy it once you have saved for it." Talk about wisdom and frugality. But isn't this the way our grandfathers and great-grandfathers did things in the 1920's and 30's before the scourge of credit card spending took us by throat, injecting its deadly venom into our bright financial futures?

It has taken some time for Melvin Powers' wisdom to sink into my head, but I am there now. And I can speak from some experience, that making a lot of money, and spending a lot of money, making a lot of money, and spending a lot of money is *not* the way to wealth but to a quick path to the lack and limitation.

"Everything that has happened was meant to because if it wasn't meant to be, it would not have happened."–Charles Prosper

Remember, Disney's Snow White and the Seven Dwarfs? Those little guys were some rich little dudes. They owned diamond and jewel mines! But did you notice the modest house in which they lived – frugality at its best! They all happily went off to their diamond mine each day singing, *"Hi ho! Hi ho! It's off to work we go!"* The 21st century version of the song of seven dwarfs for most of us who go to work, will sing, *"I owe! I owe! It's off to work I go!"*

The Third Law of Money – Pay Yourself First (Automatically)

To this third law of money, the Law of Pay Yourself First Automatically, I want to give special credit where credit is due. (This is the "good" kind of credit.) I would like to acknowledge a must-read book, or if you prefer, the must-hear audio of the phenomenal, block-busting, eye-opening bestseller, The Automatic Millionaire by David Bach (ISBN 0-7679-1410-4). If you care about the financial future of yourself and that of your loved ones you must, and I say you _must_ read this book! This book should be required reading and study in every first year high school. Much of what I will explain of what is to follow concerning automatic savings and retirement planning is taken from the principles of nationally recognized financial advisor, David Bach. The book is $19.95, so even not having the money is no excuse because your public library can order it for you. If your local branch doesn't have it, they can order it from their other branches if it is within their system. Because I spend so much time in my car, I have recently become an avid listener of important financial, success and motivational audio books in my car. The Automatic Millionaire by David Bach is also on 5 audio CD's. With the audio medium in my car, I am able to finish at least two audio books a week, that's 104 audio books a year! However, I usually wind up listening to about 50 key audio book programs repeatedly over the course of the year. Repeated listenings increases my understanding and ability to mastery. Whether you buy or borrow, get this book today!

"Luck is when preparedness meets opportunity."–Earl Nightingale

Figure 2 *The Automatic Millionaire,* David Bach. ISBN 0-7679-1410-4. $19.95. www.finishrich.com

Now let's get back to the main premise of this discussion. You must pay yourself first. You must pay yourself automatically. You must decide upon a percentage. They are 3 AUTOMATIC savings account that you will need to open and keep growing:

- Sleep-Well-At-Night 3 Months Savings (5% – 10%)

- Long Term Retirement Savings Account (10%)

- Investment Savings Account (5% – 10%)

Before I go into detail of the nature of each account, let me emphasize the why and the importance that the money be transferred from your paycheck or your checking account to the savings account that you have designated AUTOMATICALLY! Notice how this is practically the only place in this entire book where I place a word in all caps. The reason is that this is the most important secret of this savings system. You see, the U.S. government figured this out a long time ago, that the only way that they could be assured and guaranteed that citizens would send in their estimated taxes would be to AUTOMATICALLY deduct it from your payroll check. It is taken out, and you don't even feel the extraction. We've gotten used to the net and not the gross. If you were asked to write a check out to the government for these estimated deductions every pay period, human nature dictates that forgetfulness and procrastination would set in, and it would never happen.

    I used to have a problem remembering to take a portion out each month and put it into savings. Most months I would, and some months I wouldn't especially if I tried to pay everyone else first and then hope that something would be left to save after I paid everyone else. I was never successful. I eventually fell off the monthly saving bandwagon, until one day by fate or serendipity, I decided to open up a retirement account for my, at the time, 6-year old daughter, Luzemily, who is now 13 years old. I wanted to make sure that she would always have this savings accumulating for her which I would give to her when she turned 18 or began working, whichever came first. The young lady opening the savings account for us at the bank told me that we could automatically have $50 taken from my personal checking account on the 25th of each month. I said okay as it sounded like a good plan to me. The result. In 24 months, I have not missed even one deposit into her account. This is the secret of safe and secure savings. If you don't have to think about it, if it is taken out of your checking account, or if your arrange with your employer to deduct and route a given amount or percentage from your payroll check automatically to a designated savings account, you will be able to save without fail. Remember, when you set up your money to be automatically transferred, you are set up to save. Let us take a look at your three most important automatic savings accounts.

"There are limitations to what you can control, but there are no limitations to what you can accept."–
Charles Prosper

Sleep-Well-At-Night 3 Months Emergency Savings

If you are living from paycheck to paycheck with no savings, you are only 3 months away from homelessness should the worst happen – if you should temporarily lose the source of your income. I have come to believe that the people who never save are uncomfortable with having emergency savings because it feels "normal" to struggle. A great deal of people assume that this is just the way things are unless you are rich. But as we have seen, if being "rich" means making a high income, one can still lose everything, if you spend excessively and create huge debt beyond your means and income. People who don't save are like the proverbial ostrich who sticks his head in the sand. If you stick you head in the sand, one thing is for sure. You'll get you ass kicked!

There are two movies, both which have as part of its drama the theme of homelessness, both based on true stories. The first movie is <u>The Pursuit of Happiness,</u> starring Wil Smith and his 8-year son. The story centers around a man who, anxious to get ahead in life by selling a type of medical scanning equipment, gets behind on his taxes and forgets to pay an overdue bill. As a good drama would have it, his wife leaves him at the worst possible moment. With the last few hundred dollars in his bank account, the IRS seizes it, leaving him totally broke and with no savings or income from his failing equipment sales. He finds himself on the streets with his son.

The other movie is <u>Conversations With God</u>, starring Henry Czerny centers around the true story of Neale Donald Walsch who discovers God through a series unusual experiences. But before his divine revelations, he gets into a car accident, breaks his neck, and is unable to continue to work. One thing leads to another, and since he too had no emergency savings fund; he finds himself living on the streets and eating out of trash dumpsters. Both stories have a happy ending as both main characters become rich and successful. But this was the movies. Life doesn't always have a happy ending. Some people, good people and their families, wind up on the streets. This is an avoidable situation.

"Acceptance = Peace."–
Charles Prosper

Stuff happens! No one expects your spouse to leave you. No one expects to lose a job, to become hurt, sick, or unable to work. Do not become the ostrich with your head in the sand. Protect yourself with ready cash. Cash is your friend. Cash is your best friend! Cash savings allow you to say, "Take this job and shove it!" Cash savings allow you to weather the storm when you have no income coming in for months. If anything can go wrong, if may, and at the worst possible time. That's the fabric of life. It's okay to be optimistic, but it's not okay to be naive. I am very optimistic when I have a cash reserve sitting in the bank that can tide me over a year or more without having to work is there is a temporary income shortage.

When you set up this Sleep-Well-At-Night Emergency Savings, you should estimate what are your total monthly expenses then multiply this by 3. This would give you the amount of money that you would need to live off if you had no income for 3 months. If your monthly expenses are $3,000, then your goal is to save up $9,000 in savings. I usually suggest that if you have no savings, to start your first emergency-savings goal for 3 months of living expenses. Your ultimate goal should be to have enough savings to tide you over for 24 months. A percentage of your net income that should be automatically transferred each month from your checking account or your payroll account to your designated emergency savings fund should be an average equivalent of no less than 5% and ideally 10% of your net income. If you can't arrange for a percentage to be transferred each month automatically then come up with a dollar amount equivalent to the an average 5% or 10% of your income. The more months in emergency reserve you have, the more secure you are and the better you will sleep at night. I heard a great definition of wealth which is the amount of *time* that you could survive without having any working income. If you could survive for 3 months, then you would be 3 months wealthy. If you could survive 3 years, you would be 3 years wealthy. If you could survive on what you have accumulated for the rest of your life, then you would be completely financially independent. With this definition, wealth is measured by the length of time you can survive by living off your accumulated savings.

When Is It an Emergency to Use Your Cash Savings?

Here is where most people fool themselves and pretend that they don't really know what an emergency is. Let's not kid ourselves. We all know what an emergency is and what it is not. Just in case you may fall prey to pretendind, let me help you with this one. A real emergency, when it comes to using your Sleep-Well-At-Night Emergency Savings, is one where your *survival* is threatened, not just your desire to be comfortable. Right now, I will give you a definitive list:

"No one can really know if a situation is unlucky until it has played itself out."–
Charles Prosper

<u>Not</u> An Emergency
- A new computer is on sale
- The Rolex at 50% off
- Need a car new transmission
- Brother needs new furniture
- Need tuition for college
- Your mother needs a loan
- You're being sued for $1000
- Airplane tickets for Christmas
- Your car gets towed for $400
- Dental implants for $5000

<u>An Emergency</u> *(only 1 reason)*
- You have lost your source of income, or you are unable to work temporarily for some unforseen illness or accident. You will now take money out of your emergency cash account, as needed, until you've recovered and are bringing in a regular income again.

The Myth of Borrowing From Your Savings–And Putting It Back

Here is the biggest trap of savings that we may fall into. It is when we say, "I'll just borrow a few hundred dollars and put it back." It never happens that way. Once you take any money out from your emergency cash savings when it is not an emergency – even if it is a dollar – it is like pulling the small rubber stopper out of a full bathtub of water. This is the crack in the dike that will cause the levy to break. You cannot ever borrow and put back money from your savings if it is *any* thing other than the one sole reason that you started this savings in the first place which was to take care of you in a financially life-threatening situation of survival. Until you are ready to use your emergency cash savings for which it was designed. Metaphorically speaking, your savings is a pure virgin which must not be touched by any other than an emergency survival situation. To be consummated for any other reason is to violate the sanctuary of its "virginity" which has been saved up for your survival only.

Your Savings Reflect Your Self-Worth and "Money Comfort Zone"

I had a friend who told me that he could never save more than $4000. Once he achieved a level of savings of $4000, "somehow" the money just left the account. I believe that everyone has an unconscious "money comfort zone" which can actually be tied to a certain dollar amount. What I mean is this. You must become used to and comfortable with larger and larger dollar amounts in your possession than you have been accustomed to before. If you have *never* managed to save more than $1000, and if you are accustomed to having no more than a $200 balance in your checking account, this is your "money comfort zone". You will always tend to revert back to these amounts if you are unconscious that they exist. If you receive a large sum of money, you will quickly try to "get rid of it and back to your "money comfort zone."

When I used to work as a social worker many years ago, I think of a co-worker by the name of Lisa, who before she finished school and became a high-earning social worker, had lived for many years on welfare with her mother. She was very proud of the fact that she was the first in her family to finish school and begin a professional career. I once commented to her that I have always had the habit of keeping a folded $100 bill hidden in my wallet which I would never spend but to always give me a sense of having and experiencing prosperity. She laughed and said. "Ha! If I have any more than $20 sitting in *my* pocket, I'm going to *spend* it!" This was her "money comfort zone", to always walk around with no more than $20 in her pocket.

Having more money saved is almost like bodybuilding. You must learn to gradually push yourself to be able to withstand larger and larger amounts. People are not as comfortable with large sums of money

"There are no secrets to success. It is the result of preparation, hard work, learning from failure."–
General Colin L. Powell

as they would like to admit. Re-examine your life, and decide what has been your dollar-amount "money comfort zone" barrier, and push yourself to withstand larger amounts than you have ever accumulated and do whatever it takes to withstand the temporary "discomfort" of having more money than you are used to. You will get used to it, and it will soon feel natural to you and become a part of your permanent "financial consciousness."

Long Term Retirement Automatic Savings Account

How old are you? You don't have to really tell me. I just want *you* to think about it for a moment. Your desire and awareness of the importance of a long term retirement savings account should be a direct reverse-relationship to how young you are. What I mean is, if you are 21 years old and fresh out of college, and let's say that you have already begun your career and are making a healthy beginning salary of $70,000 the chances are that retirement planning is probably the last thing on your mind. You probably have decided that you are too young to think about this right now; you have worked too hard studying all those years getting your diploma. Now it's time for you to enjoy your life a little is the thought. Right? "I need my high definition TV, my 'jag', and I absolutely must dress in the best style. Hey! I deserve it, don't I? All this retirement stuff can come much later."

"Life affords no higher pleasure than that of surmounting difficulties."—Samuel Johnson

Usually most people start to wake up and think about retirement, if at all, in their late 30's or mid-40's when it has become a little late in the game. Hitting age 50, panic starts to set in, and there begins a race to catch up. It is never to late to start however, but the later you start the more creative and proactive you will have to be with yours savings, investment and entrepreneurial strategies. Remember, it is never too late to start, but it is always better to start as early as possible. My daughter is only thirteen years old, and I have already started her automatic retirement savings account. I am not going to be around forever, and I want to make sure that she learns good money skills early and will be adequately taken care of when I am gone and not have to depend upon any man to take care of her.

My suggestion is that you run, don't walk and seek out the recommendation of a reliable and succesful person that you know and trust who could give you the recommendation of a good financial planner. You need to sit down with an expert and draw up a long term retirement financial strategy. This means, decide upon a target date when you feel that you would like to retire or semi-retire with a healthy savings nest egg. This could be in the next 10 years, 20 years, 30 years or 40 years. The longer the time you have the better. Remember, if you do nothing, and if you are still alive, the next 10, 20, 30 or 40 years will pass anyway whether you do something with your life or not.

I am saying do *something!* Anything! $100,000 in retirement is better than nothing. $100,000 is even better. $250,000 better. $300,000 – now we're talking. The secret to retirement savings is setting up something like an IRA (Individual Savings Account) that pays compound interest – which is when the bank adds to your savings and increases your balance as it pays you interest on the original balance *plus* the added balance! Depending on your interest rate, with just $100 monthy, you you create a surprising nest egg for yourself. Look at the chart below:

Compound Interest by Automatically Saving $100 Per Month

Interest Rate	5 Years	10 Years	15 Years	20 Years	25 Years	30 Years	35 Years	40 Years
$100/mo saved at 2.0%	$6,315	$13,294	$21,006	$29,529	$38,947	$49,355	$60,856	$73,566
$100/mo saved at 3.0%	$6,481	$14,009	$22,754	$32,912	$44,712	$58,419	$74,342	$92,837
$100/mo saved at 4.0%	$6,652	$14,774	$24,691	$36,800	$51,584	$69,636	$91,678	$111,590
$100/mo saved at 5.0%	$6,829	$15,593	$26,840	$41,275	$59,799	$83,573	$114,083	$153,238
$100/mo saved at 6.0%	$7,012	$16,470	$29,227	$49,435	$69,646	$100,954	$143,183	$200,145
$100/mo saved at 7.0%	$7,201	$17,409	$31,881	$52,397	$81,480	$122,709	$181,156	$264,012
$100/mo saved at 8.0%	$7,397	$18,417	$34,835	$59,295	$95,737	$150,030	$230,918	$351,428
$100/mo saved at 9.0%	$7,599	$19,497	$38,124	$67,290	$112,953	$184,447	$296,385	$471,643
$100/mo saved at 10.0%	$7,808	$20,655	$41,792	$76,570	$133,789	$227,933	$382,828	$637,678
$100/mo saved at 11.0%	$8,025	$21,899	$45,886	$87,357	$159,058	$283,023	$497,347	$867,896
$100/mo saved at 12.0%	$8,249	$23,234	$50,458	$99,915	$189,764	$352,991	$649,527	$1,188,242

"Gratitude is prayer." –
Charles Prosper

Now this is a chart with an example of a mininmal savings plan of only $100 per month. Can you imagine what your financial picture would look like if you were to save, say, $300 per month, $500 per month or $1,200 per month? This type of savings is possible if in a two income household, you would live on one income and save all of the other's.

Investment Automatic Savings Account

This is another automatic savings account which I like to call your financial freedom account. This is the account where you order 5% to 10% of your income to be sent to a savings account that you will use for the purpose of invested in some type of business that will produce passive income for you. Passive income means that this is income that, once you set it up, it will keep producing money for you. The internet is a great place to start. People are making lots of money with many types of internet businesses that you can start. Coin operated vending machines is another example of passive income. Selling on eBay is a way to passive income streams, and of course rental real estate is the big one, once you have adequately studied the subject and have saved up enough money to invest. I am just scratching the surface here when it comes to all of the thousands of part-time business opportunities out there. As a start, I would suggest that you start reading the business opportunity magazines sold on the newsstand like Entrepreneur and Business Opportunites. You will find many possibilities to your liking. Always choose a business that appeals to you on a heart-felt level. With this savings, you are never to spend it on anything that does not have the purpose to start a new income stream for you.

"Always aim for achievement, and forget about success." –Helen Hayes

Everyone Should Have Some Type of Part-Time Business

This statement is highly opinionated. It is my high opinion. I have come to the conclusion that unless you adopt of the mindset of creating multiple streams of income for yourself, you will always be locked in a fixed prison of salary which you are earning. Another thing is that no job, no matter how high the salary, is *guaranteed*. You may be making $150,000 a year in a high-paying salaried job, and get used to that high salary lifestyle. You may lose yourself in all of the self-indulgent trappings that go along with assuaging your ego, e.g., the big mortgage, the luxury car payment, the fancy clothes, and the ritzy restaurants. "I am sorry, Mr. Thomas, but we will have to downsize due to a fall in our stock, and regretfully we will have to lay you off." Everything else that is said after that becomes a blur.

When you start multiple streams of income by creating a manageable part-time home-based business, you could even later become a full-time entrepreneur should you choose. This is thinking with wealth-consciousness, through self-reliance, by not depending on a paycheck.

Whose knows. Maybe one day you will wake up excitedly and say, "I love my job. I love my boss. Because I'm self-employed!"

Multiple Streams of Income – The Parthenon of Financial Security

Take a look at this illustration of a Greek parthenon. If you look closely, you will notice that it's architectural design and structural integrity is based on the multiple pillars which support it.

Figure 3 The Greek parthenon is the metaphor of your financial security through multiple streams of income.

"You never suffer from a money problem; you always suffer from an idea problem."–Robert H. Schuller

Think in terms of each new income stream that you create for yourself like the Greek parthenon that will support you even if one of the pillars fall. If your only income stream is your job, then you can see what type of parthenon you are supporting. If you lose your job, then the structure of your life falls on top of you. Think of it like this, the more income streams that you have, the more pillars have you that support your financial security. If you are sales-oriented and love working with people, joining a reputable network marketing company could be an excellent way for you to create another stream of income for yourself. Wealthy people and businessmen do this all of the time. They call it diversifying their money. I have heard it said that you should aim for as many as seven different multiple streams of income in your life which should take away the fear concerning the issue of job security.

The Fourth Law of Money - You Must <u>*Enjoy*</u> Money to Increase It

Making money is not just about saving money, you must learn to truly enjoy money to increase more of it into your life. This is part of the spiritual law of attraction. Whatever you enjoy or whatever you fear – you attract more of it. It is here that I say to you – enjoy money! Truly enjoy it, but do it within the guise of your savings plans already mentioned.

Here I take a different tact and say that you should also save a "mad money" account. With this account, you could save a percentage automatically sent to a savings account from your checking account, or you could simply, at the end of the day, throw all of your loose change and a few dollar bills into a mad money jar. The idea is that every month, you will "blow" all of the money on something that you would normally would not give yourself the permission to do, such as taking yourself out to the most luxurious hotel in your area, and stay over night, or dine out in the finest restaurant; this you could do alone, or you can share the experience with a friend. The idea is to get used to the feeling of enjoying money, for more money will be attracted to you. If you only have ten dollars to your name, take one of those dollars, and think of a way to truly _enjoy_ it, if it is no more than buying an ice cream cone or taking a long trolley ride. Whatever you do, make sure that you _enjoy_ it!

"Nothing can bring you peace but yourself."–Ralph Waldo Emerson

The Fifth Law of Money - You Must _Give_ Money to Increase It

This idea of giving money, and the idea of giving in and of itself for the sheer pleasure of giving is so important that I have devoted an entire chapter is to this subject. Suffice it to say that when you give more to help and improve the quality of life of other people less fortunate than you, your money will increase. I can only say, try it, and then see what happens.

The Sixth Law of Money - You Must _Invest_ Money to Increase It

We touched upon this law in the discussion of creating an automatic investment retirement savings. We talked about the importance of starting some type of additional home-based part-time businesses for yourself, and we discoursed on the importance of creating multiple streams of income just as the ancient Greek parthenon was created to stand firmly and solidly with multiple pillars. But always remember. Invest in businesses and services that are closest to your heart, and the things that you love to do, and the things that you value the most.

The Seventh Law of Money - Be _Grateful_ for Money to Increase It

Yes, gratitude is the attitude, the one that puts you closest to God's heart. It is important to know that you must be grateful before you have a lot of money as well as grateful after you have the money in your life. Gratitude sets all sorts of positive forces into motion, creative ideas being only one of them. Remember, it is not how much you have, but how much you enjoy that creates happiness. The more gratitude that you feel, the more joy you will feel and the more happiness will be your experience.

"You are not only who you are today but also who you choose to become tomorrow."–
Melvin Powers

CHAPTER 12

The Law of Gratitude

The Law of Gratitude is the law of happiness. There is always an immediate reward for gratitude, and that reward is the joy for that which we are thankful. If anyone wants a quick and guaranteed recipe for instant happiness, I just say count your blessings. This is not a new idea. Some might even say that it is just common sense, but again, how *common* is "common" sense? I would like to propose a methodical and very effective daily practice for you to reap the benefits of giving thanks.

The Gratitude Diary – Recording Your Blessings One by One

I challenge you to practice what I am going to tell you for only 30 days, and I'll bet you'll get hooked on it and will not want to stop. You will begin to attract "good luck", prosperity, health and peace of mind. For 30 days, either once in the morning or once in the evening, I want you to number, write down and record at least 10 things that you will recognize and be thankful for, no matter how "small" or how big on the surface it might seem. Life in itself is a miracle, and there are no insignificant things in God's universe.

    First, I would like for you to go out to your nearest stationery or drug store and purchase a spiral notebook which you will used exclusively for your Gratitude Diary. If you want a suggestion in notebooks that I have found nice for this practice it is the Mead® Five Star® Premier spiral notebook which measures about 6.75"wide x 9.5" high. It contains about 200 pages, and they usually come in an assortment of colors. My favorite color is blue.

    You open the first page, and on the top line at the upper left hand side, you write the date. Skip a line, then in the middle of the page, you write "Entries". Skip another line, and then begin to number all the good that happened to you during that day if you are recording before you go to bed, or you can record all the good that happened to you the day before or anything that you can recognize in your life right now, if you happen to be recording this upon awakening and before you start your day. It is alright is you repeat certain things again and again each day. That thing that you are repeating and writing over and over again will only tend to appear more and more in your life. I leave what you write and how often you write it up to you.

"The grateful mind continually expects good things, and expectation becomes faith." –Wallace D. Wattles

Figure 4 Here I am making a daily entry into my Gratitude Diary.

This is how I would suggest that you make your entries. Start out with the phrase, "I am grateful and thankful for…" After "for" at the elipsis, fill in whatever it is you would like to recognize:

1. *I am grateful and thankful for* the checker game I played with my 8-year old daughter.
2. *I am grateful and thankful for* the informative book I found on real estate investing.
3. *I am grateful and thankful for* the 3 lbs. I lost through eating better.
4. *I am grateful and thankful for* the fragrance of honeysuckle through my bedroom window each night.
5. *I am grateful and thankful for* my new patience with people.

And so on and so forth. You get the idea.

Now there are two ways to give thanks and recognition for the good things in your life through your Gratitude Diary. One way is to recognize and to be thankful for all that you have, but, and here is the secret. You can also use your Gratitude Diary to be thankful for all that which you believe that will come. There is magic in thanking in advance.

Gratitude is Prayer

What is prayer? Prayer is an attractive magnetic force that brings you what you ask when it is interceded by God, Higher Power, The Universe, All-That-Is or whatever label you would attempt to place on the Creative and Integrating Intelligence that organizes all life. Gratitude is prayer that becomes faith, and faith moves mountains. The more you are thankful ahead of time, and in writing, the more you will be thankful

"Bless you and thank you is synonymous!" –Charles Prosper

again in writing (and in your heart) once it has manifested. To turn your Gratitude Diary into a prayer book, think of the things that you would like to appear in your life and affirm:
1. *I am grateful and thankful for* the solution to my problem of..."
2. *I am grateful and thankful for* the spontaneous healing of my..."
3. *I am grateful and thankful for* being debt free.
4. *I am grateful and thankful for* finding my soul mate.
5. *I am grateful and thankful for* my new patience with people.

Keep going until you get to 10 or 20 items, or write as many items as you want or have time for.

Gratitude is Magnetic

The power of gratitude is the Law of Attraction in action. When you are grateful for something, you are unwittingly loving it. You attract that which you love. Being grateful is true spiritual love versus the silly romantic love that we tend to think of when we first hear the word. When you are thankful, you are loving, and when you are either thankful are loving, you are placing yourself close to the heart of God. For God hears best from those whose lips come the words that are carried by the wings of gratefulness.

"I am blessed to the degree that I recognize that I am already blessed."–Charles Prosper

Gratitude Prospers You

All of the goodness and bounty of life is yours the minute that you can accentuate the positive, eliminate the negative and don't even bother with whatever might be in between. Not only will prosperity follow you if you are thankful before it even before it appears, but you will be given the immediate feeling of peace and pleasure that it is on its way. This feeling of peace is your faith in God to grant you all that you are asking as you believe and feel it to be so even before your physical eyes can proclaim its reality when its reality. Reality resides as the primal cause in the realm of the invisible.

"Faith is the substance of things hoped for, the evidence of things not see."–Hebrews 11:1

Once Every 30 Days, Re-Read All of Your Entries

Every 30 days, set aside 30 minutes to re-read as much of your diary as you can. You can read from front to back, or you can jump around and read page to page. You will be surprised at how many things you are reading will have already happened.

I am thankful and grateful for your having read this chapter.

"You are not only who you are today but also who you choose to become tomorrow."–
Melvin Powers

CHAPTER 13

The Law of Giving

God is a giver, and He wants to give to and needs to give to you, through you, to others. When God has given you a talent or ability He expects for you to give it to others on His behalf. Giving and receiving, as all enlightened people see, are just the two sides of the same gold coin. You cannot give without receiving because your giving will always result in an immediate sense of a peace that passes all understanding.

> *"God gives to the giver and takes from the taker."*
> —Reverend Frederick Eikerenkoetter

And you cannot outgive God. Just try it sometimes. Start giving for the sheer joy of giving – and God will match you by giving you even more in your life.

"Okay, God, let's play," you say.

"Okay, my son, you're on!" replies God.

In the end, God will always outgive you. Why? Because His love is infinite as his gifts are infinite. But the game is fun anyway. Go ahead. Play it and enjoy it!

Sharing is Having More

This is true on so many levels, but none is more immediately apparent than when you share something with a stranger who is not expecting it. Let me give you an example. I love fine chocolate of at least 65% cocao. One day when I was checking out a couple of books at my local bookstore, I saw some fine 65% cocao near the check out counter. I asked that the clerk include it along with my purchase of the books. The clerk did so, and continue to process the rest of my book order. I quickly opened up the chocolate wrapper exposing a two inch square of pure chocolate delight.

"Here, please have some chocolate," I offered the busy cashier totaling up the order. He hesistated. Somewhat startled and in semi-disbelief. Suddenly a smile broke through. Then his whole face lit up as he "courageously" extended his hand to break off a piece.

"Why, *thank* you! How did you know I love chocolate?"

"I didn't. Just thought you deserved a moment of enjoyment."

"The greatest gift God can give you is the gift you give to others." –Charles Prosper

"Have a great, evening, sir, and come back and visit us soon."
"Will do," I smiled and I waved goodbye.

How do you think the favor of the rest of that chocolate piece tasted to me after that sharing moment? I can only say that the chocolate appeared to taste even *better*–better than if I had eaten the entire bar! I later wrote that in my Gratitude Diary, "*I am thankful and grateful for the cashier with whom I shared a piece of chocolate.*"

The Secret of Attracting Good Luck Everyday of Your Life

I have always suspected this, but it was not until recently that I tried it out and then again, and then again and then again. And now I have come to the definitive conclusion that there *is* a secret to creating your own good luck. The secret is to find something that you can anonymously do for another person where they, or no one else, will ever find out who it was. Now the secret is to *anonymously* give or help another. I know that it feels good to do something for someone and expect to hear the thanks and gratitude that follows, but when you give and wait to be thanked, then their thanks becomes your reward, and their is nothing wrong with that. But when you don't say anything to anyone then God steps in to thank *you*. When God says thanks, He does it with style and does so lavishly. Now there is a pitfall if you are not careful. Your motive for giving must be for the sheer joy of giving because you know that it is just a good thing to do. You cannot cajole or manipulate God.

"Okay, God, I just helped this guy out. Whataya gonna' *give* me? Come on, God, stop the stallin'."

Your giving must be as natural "*...as in yonder valley the myrtle breathes its fragrance into space...*"–Kahlil Gibran (The Prophet). It must be given from heart to heart.

I give you a challenge. Just try doing something for someone or giving something to someone, and do it so that you never tell anyone – ever! You will be amazed at the good luck and "coincidences" that will come your way! The word "coincidence" doesn't explain the *why*. We often feel comfortable when we can just *label* things even though we do not understand them. How often does a "coincidence" have to happen before God is given the credit. "Coincidence" is the language of God. "Coincidence is how God speaks to us.

Do some good for someone today anonymously, be itbig or small. You will begint to attract good luck to yourself. Try it.

The Mystery Jogger

Let me tell you a story. It is a story of a mystery morning jogger. Every other morning at about 4:30 a.m., just before dawn on a quiet city street of a quiet neighborhood in the Los Feliz area of Los Angeles, a

"We make a living by what we earn–we make a life by what we give."–Winston Churchill

mystery jogger would ready himself for his pre-dawn mile run. In a moment, you will see why I call him the Mystery Jogger. He asked me that he remain anonymous. He shared this interesting true story with me in the hopes of maybe inspiring others to do similar deeds.

It is time for the morning mile run. The sun rises in about an hour. He ties his running shoes, and attaches his iPod around the biceps of his left sleeve. He pushes the on button. "Momma, come here quick, and gimme that lickin' stick..." the rhythmic, "Lickin' Stick" song by James Brown. He's off.

The cool morning breeze blows gently onto his face as the trees and parked cars whiz by in a soft blur in his peripheral vision. He knows that he is only about five blocks away. Five blocks away, he will encounter the unknown homeless guy who sleeps every night on the streets, covered with dirty, smelly clothes, and under a grimy plaid blanket in the doorway of a closed print shop. The Mystery Jogger's footsteps tap the concrete pavement as he runs. Faster. Faster. *Thud. Thud. Thud.* The sound gently echoes throughout the silence street of the pre-dawn morning.

"There he is!" The Mystery Jogger sees the unknowned homeless guy, as usual, lying in the doorway of the printshop dreaming of only-God-knows-what just before he wakes for another day of hoping that life will be not as bad as yesterday and maybe just a whee bit better today. So, on with our story.

The Mystery Jogger is now right over the sleeping man. He reaches into his jogging-pants pocket, and pulls out about twenty dollars in one dollar bills, and throws the paper money gently in a corner near the sleeping man's face, such that when he awakes, he will surely feel that he was visited in his dreams by an angel of God. One never knows when dreams will come true.

What this mystery jogger told me is that the 'high" and the feeling of joy that he gets when he does that starts his morning on the right foot, and snowballs into nothing but good feelings all day. He told me that as a result of this practice, he was given what he believes was a divine multi-million idea that will change his life. He also notices that there is striking correlation (coincidence if you will) to all of the unexpected money that shortly comes into his life. He told me that even if none of these good things immediately followed, giving in anonymity and knowing that one is doing the right thing would be enough for him. Nevertheless, prosperity keeps on pouring into his life non-stop. What could you do to help someone anonymously? Maybe you could send a rent payment to a family who is about to be evicted? Can you imagine what you might reap from such an act of selfless giving?

To Whom Do You Give Your Time?

"We cannot do great things on this earth. We can only do small things with great love." –Mother Teresa

Some people say time is money. I would also like to say that in some instances giving your time is much more important than giving your money.

Do you give your time to your loved ones, or do you give it mostly to your job, career or your pursuit of success while neglecting your loved ones? Giving also means giving your time which can be as valuble or even more so tht the commodity we call money. It is funny but you never hear anyone on their death bed say, " I just wish I could have spent a little more time in the office or a little more time returning calls to customers. You always hear something like, "If I had only just spent a little more time with my family. If I could have only been there for her when my daughter or son was growing up. If I had just called and told my father how much I loved him and appreciated him before he died." *If. If. If.*

I only want to ask you 3 questions. 3 powerful questions.

If you had only 1 hour to live:

1) Who would you call?

2) What would you say?

And the third and most important question of them all —

3) <u>Why</u> are you waiting?

I would like to give you an assignment of giving. Think of 3 very important persons in your life. It could be family or friends. Call these 3 people today, and tell them how much you appreciate them. Do it now. You have the cell phone. Use it properly.

Can You Play with Me Daddy?

I will never forget the time when my daughter, Luzemily, was about 5-years old when she asked me one evening as I was transfixed on the computer screen answering emails of clients, "Can you play with me, Daddy?" I retorted to her, "No, Luzemily, I'm too busy, baby." Suddenly a sickly feeling overcame me as I saw her tear-filled eyes staring back at me and said, "Okay, daddy." In the saddest tone you can imagine. I stopped dead in my tracks with tears now in *my* eyes as I turned off the computer immediately, stood up and said, "Yes, baby, of *course*, I'll play with you."

I may have thought at the time that those email customers were important, but they weren't. I don't even remember who they were, and frankly I don't care. However, I vowed from that night that I would

"I long to accomplish a great and noble task, but it is my chief duty to accomplish small tasks as if they were great and noble." –Helen Keller

never–*ever*–deny my daughter of my time–even if it was only 10 minutes. If I can't stop and give my baby *10 stinkin' minutes of my time,* I don't deserve to have her! Since that time, I've never allowed myself to believe I am too busy or too important to stop a moment and give her some time whenever she requests it. No one needs to work that hard until values are displaced.

When our children leave the nest, we are left with only the memories we have made. If they are good ones there will be no regrets. Giving creates peace, and peace produce happiness. The ultimate goal of everything that we do, whether we realize it or not is to obtain peace. Even when we seek pleasure, which is not the same a peace, we are hoping that after the satisfaction of the urge for any given pleasure, we will be led to a state of peace. Depending on how that which is to give is given, sometimes peace will follows, and sometimes not. When you give from the heart, expecting nothing in return, is your guarantee of the peace that you seek.

"Common sense is instinct. Enough of it is genius."–
George Bernard Shaw

We could not end our discussion of giving without touching upon the subject of tithing. If you have heard of the concept of tithing at all, it was probably in a religious setting of your church, mosque or synagogue. True tithing is a spiritual principle, and it does have one distinct advantage – it works! The etymology of the word tithe is tenth. This is the ancient practice is giving the first tenth of your harvest or earnings to the church. I am not advocating or proselytizing any particular religion, for that is a personal choice, but I can say that the practice of regularly and automatically giving to any worthy cause that you believe it will do wonders for you and the organization to whom you give. The first benefit of giving charitably is that you begin to *feel* wealthy, as one who has. What you feel, by the Law of Attraction expands more into your life. Therefore, if by giving, you feel more powerful and prosperous, you will begin to become so. It may start with your receiving more money-making ideas, or it may be through the attraction of more of the right people in your life who can help you progress and prosper more.

Tithing is not necessarily about any given percentage. It is really about giving for the joy of giving. You could start with 1%, 2% or 3% of your take home pay, and gradually work up to 10% as you see the results of giving. One last thing, to whichever organization you choose to give, be it your church or synagogue or a non-profit organization, arrange with your bank automatically transfer the money.

"You are not only who you are today but also who you choose to become tomorrow."–
Melvin Powers

Part II

Practical Applications of the Laws of Success

"You are not only who you are today but also who you choose to become tomorrow."–
Melvin Powers

CHAPTER 14

How to Overcome Procrastination

Unless you overcome procrastination, the putting off of important and necessary things until some later date, you cannot succeed at anything you say you want to achieve. This is so important, let me say it again. Unless you overcome procrastination, you absolutely cannot succeed at anything!

Procrastination is the Root of Failure

Procrastination is at the root of all failure, and procrastination is always selective. We procrastinate on somethings, and will conscientiously follow through without hesitation on others. I am a born-again non-procrastinator. This is something that, after seeing all the harm and damage it had caused in my life, I finally decided that I would do whatever it took to never procrastinate on important things again. To give you an example of how selective procrastination used to work in my life, I would procrastinate in doing my income taxes, many times I would go beyond the allotable limit and wind up paying late fees and penalties. On the other hand, when it came to my exercise program, I had absolutely no problem in getting up at 4:00 a.m. in the morning and go outside in my garden, sometimes in 30º degree weather and work out with weights for an hour before starting my workday. Some people would selectively procrastinate on going out in the pre-dawn to do an exercise program while others would chose to do their taxes on time. That's why I say that procrastination is selective.

We unwittingly decide, below a full awareness of consciousness what we think is doable and what we think is not. If we unconsciously believe that a task is extremely difficult, we will tend to postpone it. If an executioner gave you the choice of having your head chopped off today or to wait until next week, which would you choose? The problem is that all of our *"postponed executions"* (of the important and necessary tasks of our lives that depend on whether or not we will be successful) are all *imaginary.* Here is where most people go into denial. By the selective nature of our procrastination, in that we will accomplish some things well and on time, yet other things of equal or greater importance, we wait until a later date leads us to believe that procrastination is not a big problem at all. Let me ask you a very important question:

"Putting off an easy thing makes it hard. Putting off a hard thing makes it impossible."–George Claude Lorimer

Have you wanted to be, do or have something in your life for a long time and still don't have it? If your answer to this question is no, then you too are probably a procrastinator! You are letting your dreams die, and there is nothing worst in life that you can do to yourself than that! Take heart. My purpose in saying this is not to brow beat you. I want to help. I want to show you before you finish this chapter, proven ways to be, do and have what you want by showing you how to conquer the monster of procrastination forever! Read now, my friend. Don't procrastinate.

"Success is Doing What You Say You Will Do"

This is a saying that I got from my dear mother, and I think that it is the simplest and the best definition of success that I have ever heard. You see, most of us have a pretty good idea of *what* to do, to intitiate the solving of our problems, but it is the *doing* that gets in the way.

We live in an information age. We can obtain the know-how, if we look hard enough and long enough, through books, audio CD's, community college courses and online internet instruction on anything! So lack of knowledge is not the problem. Knowledge, or the how-to of anything surrounds us, but ironically sometimes procrastination will stop us from even reading and studying the very book that has the answers. Let me give you an example. One day I was studying in the public library near my home with my daughter, Luzemily. A young lady, probably in her mid-twenties, a worker in the library whose job is to organize and shelve the books passed near our table and commented on how she would see my daughter and I in the library every afternoon studying for a couple of hours after work.

"I see you and your daughter here everyday. She must be quite a student."

As a proud papa would respond, "Yes, she is an all A-student, and she won student of the month at her school in April."

"What grade are you in?" the young lady askes Luzemily.

"Third grade," my daughter answers.

"And what do you want to be when you grow up?"

"A doctor," Luzemily replies without hesistation.

"How interesting! I too want to be a doctor, but I am first studying to be a nurse, in case becoming a doctor doesn't work out."

I nearly went crazy when I heard here say that. "If you don't mind my saying, but that type of thinking will *never* get you to become a doctor. You have got to *commit*. You have to be willing to do whatever it takes. You have to truly *believe* in yourself and your goal."

"Yeah, I guess your right," she says with an embarrassed smile.

"May I make a suggestion to you of an excellent book that is also on DVD?"

"Getting an idea should be like sitting on a pin; it should make you jump up and do something."–E.L. Simpson

"Sure," she said.

"It is called 'The Secret' by Rhonda Byrne. It is available in book, DVD and audio CD. Since you work here in the library, you can probably obtain it very easily through this library. Let's go take a look right now."

We all walk over to the checkout desk where she finds a computer that is not occupied. "I really enjoyed the DVD version. It is quite emotional and breathetaking," I said.

"Okay, I'll see if I can find a copy of the DVD."

She types in the information to request the availability. She sees that she would be number 102 on the waiting list!

"Wow! I didn't realize that 'The Secret' was so popular."

"Well," I suggested, "I saw a copy of the DVD on the shelves of the Video Hut a couple of blocks down the street. I can call right now and have them reserve you a copy."

I then take out my cell phone and dial.

"Video Hut, may I help you?"

"Yes, would you have a spare copy of the DVD 'The Secret' on your shelves?"

"Yes, we do."

"Can you hold that copy for me?"

"Sure. Under what name?"

"Prosper. A friend of mine will be picking it up today."

"Gotcha."

"Thank you."

"You're welcome."

I turn to our young lady, "They will hold it for you for a day."

"Um. Well. I don't think can get today. I'll have to pass over and get it tomorrow. Maybe it will be there tomorrow afternoon when I have a chance to stop by."

I was somewhat puzzled by her response. All she had to do was to go three blocks down the street and pick it up. So the unconditional "giver" in me kicks in as I think, *"What's the big deal, I will just buy her a copy and give it to her tomorrow."* I later that day get her the DVD of "The Secret".

Next day, I go over excitedly to give her gift. She is not working this day, so I ask one of her co-workers to take the large envelope with the DVD inside and give it to her when she comes back to work the next day.

Just so happened that I did not see her until three weeks later when Luzemily and I walked in to find our usual table for study.

"Oh, Mr. Prosper, thank you so much for the DVD. I was so surprised to get it!"

"Well," anxious to ask, "how did you like it?"

"This one makes a net; this one stands and wishes. Would you like to make a bet, which one gets the fishes?" –Chinese rhyme

"Well, I haven't had a chance to look at it yet. I've been so busy with my studies and all."

I was dismayed, and I understood something that I had noticed many times in the past, but for the first time, with this incidence, it was very clear to me. Unless someone is willing to do whatever it takes, procrastination will take precedence and determine the outcome.

How Much Do You *Want* to Overcome Procrastination?

I have come to the conclusion that conquering procrastination really comes down to desire. How much do you *want* to become a non-procrastinator? Now put it in the first person, "How much do *I* want to become a non-procrastinator?" Have you made becoming a non-procrastinator a written goal? You should. Have you gone through the 7 Goal-Achievement Formula explained in Chapter 2 to become a non-procrastinator? Refer back to page 18. Do it now! Go through the 7 steps to overcome procrastination – *right now!*

Why Do We Procrastinate?

Before I explain to you why we procrastinate, let me make something perfectly clear. Procrastination has nothing to do with you being a lazy or an irresponsible person because nobody procrastinates with *everything!* I want to keep this simple. The cause of procrastination is always based on some kind of "fear of failure". That's it. It is no more complicated than that.

> *"Not everything that is faced can be changed, but nothing can be changed until it is faced."*
> *–James Baldwin*

The solution is equally as simple. You must dogheadedly *do* whatever it is that you fear, and death of the fear is certain. This may not be something that you will accomplish all at once or even on the first few tries, but if you *refuse* to give up in your quest to end procrastination, you will end it.

The Procrastination of Perfectionism (Fear of Self-Criticism)

Proscrastination is triggered by the neurotic and insidious practice of perfectionism which says, "If I can't do this perfectly then I won't do it at all." How sick is *that?* What on earth can anybody do *perfectly*–as though a state of perfection existed somewhere on Earth. An offshoot of this irrational idea is putting onself in a perpetual "*state-of-getting-ready*". This is none the less prevalent with career college students, especially many of those who major in business. I know that many young people study business administration primarily as an excuse not

"The rewards in business go to the man who does something with an idea." –W.H. Auden

to get started and go out in the real world and take a chance and some real-life risks for business success. They can't start a business because they "need" an MBA. And then once the MBA is achieved, they "need" more postgraduate studies, then maybe some specialized courses, and it goes on *ad infinitum, ad nauseum.* The perpetual state of getting ready is the alibi to not having to do something now.

I am thinking now of a young lady studying business who was in that exact predicament. After talking with her on the phone for 15 minutes, she saw the light, and later sent me the email below.

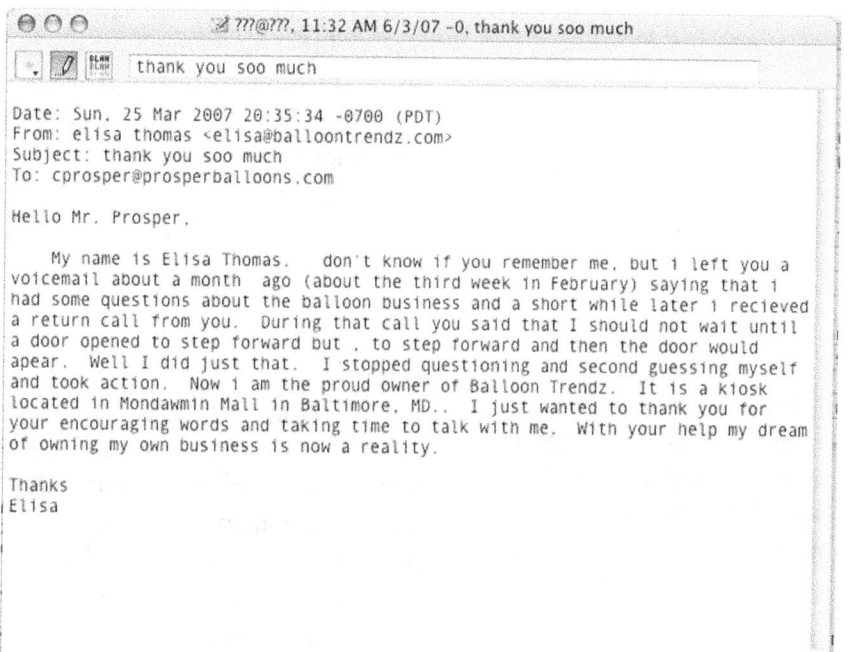

"The prayer of the chicken hawk does not get him the chicken."—Swahili proverb

Figure 5 This is the testimonial letter I received from Elisa Thomas upon her understanding how procrastination was holding her back.

The Procrastination of Overwhelm (Fear of Failure)

Proscrastination that is triggered by overhwhelm says, "If I can't do it easily, then I won't do it at all." My answer to that is "Anything worth doing is worth doing *lousy.* Just do *something*–anything! Make corrections later." I've got a news bulletin. Life ain't easy! Stuff happens. Problems arise. Difficulties exist. To hide from problems is to hide from life. I will go into specific techniques of "procrastination-busting" a little later in this chapter, but for now, I can tell you that the way to conquer the procrastination of overwhelm is to take the simplest and most obvious thing that you can do, and begin with that. If what you must do involves calling the IRS, start by *getting out the phone number.*

The Procrastination of Disapproval (Fear of Rejection)

There are so many things that you will have to do in spite of the disapproval of others that I don't even know where to begin. If you hesitate to do what you must do because of the possibility that others may or may not approve of what you do will keep you in a paralyzed state of inaction, and you will never by happy. It is not what others think of you. It is always about what *you* think of you! This is what defines an adult versus a child. And please don't to tell me that it is because you are shy.

Shyness Sucks

I have never met a shy leader, a shy champion athlete, a shy millionaire, or a shy politician. How about a shy salesperson? Shyness is for followers. Life's doors open for the bold and the courageous. Shy people are good people, however, they are just not the vanguards of the world. It's okay to have fear–but you must act in spite of that fear. You must have at least the *intention* to conquer the fear. Successful people have fears. The only difference is that they feel the fear–*and do it anyway!* If you know that you must make a call. Make the call! Poop in your pants if you must, but make that call. I guarantee, that after you have made the dreaded call, you will feel a little braver and stronger for the next time. And the next. And the next. And the next. Your poopy pants experience will also have diminished and disappeared forever.

If you know that you deserve that raise. *Ask for it!* Force yourself even as your knees knock and your body trembles. But don't run! If you want to ask that pretty lady for her phone number in the cosmetics department, strike up a casual conversation about the perfume for your cousin, then just *ask her* for the number. Rejection is good! Rejection is sweet! Rejection is wonderful! Why? Because it *frees* you if you let it. If your fear no rejection, then what becomes possible for you? *Everything!* If that's not total freedom, then I don't know what is.

Now, I would like to become very practical with you and offer you 12 time tested methods for getting rid of procrastination from you life–*permanently!*

The 12 Steps to Total "Procrastination-Busting"

If you faithfully follow what I am about to offer you, can say adios to procrastination for good.

1. **Set the Task and Move *Fast!***

2. **Be Willing to Suffer Intially.**

3. **Visualize Yourself Doing the Task Easily .**

4. **Create and Carry Around a Goal Card.**

"You've got to get to the stage in life where going-for-it is more important than winning or losing." –Arthur Ashe

5. Write Down a To-Do List the Night Before.

6. Repeat "Do it now!" 10 Times before the Task.

8. Refuse to Make Excuses.

9. Begin with a Detailed Plan.

10. Eat an Elephant.

11. Start with the Most Difficult Task First.

12. Make an *Appointment* with Yourself.

Step 1: Set the Task and Move *Fast!*

In chapter 2, you already learned the importance of setting goals to achieve anything worthwhile. Guess what? You will now set the goal to overcome your procrastination of important tasks, and make it a number 1 priority goal.

Once you have established whatever it is that you have decided to be an important thing to achieve, the next step is to *create a fast tempo*. Start putting whatever it is into action fast– with a sense of urgency–as though the house were on fire and your doing of the goal depended on your extinguishing a fire before any futher damage could be caused. Maintain a *fast tempo* as you do what you must do. A fast tempo is essential to "procrastination busting" and your success. Work at a brisk pace. Walk quickly. Move quickly. Write quickly. Speed up every action that you must do. Working fast creates a feeling of flow, and working fast bypasses the initial resistance of inertia. Once you get going fast and break inertia, your tendency is to keep going. Soon you will see that the effort is subsiding. You are now on automatic pilot.

How many times you have dragged yourself into the gym onto the workout floor, not in the mood to do anything. If you suddenly start to move fast, to set up your weights, get out your exercise workout book, grab a sets of weights, and begin without too much thought, you will notice that a momentum has started and begins to pick up. Once you start, after a few minutes of sticking with it, you will be able to quickly move pass the inertia barrier. From this point, you are happily doing your exercises.

"The biggest sin is sitting on your ass."–Florynce Kennedy

" 'Mean to' don't pick no cotton."–*Anonymous*

Step 2: Be Willing to Suffer Initially

Overcoming the intial inertia of procrastination is not easy. This is where many people become shocked and discouraged. Overcoming the inertia of procrastination is painful! Know this now, and accept it! Go into the task with the idea of a martyr. "I am going to suffer. I am willing to suffer. I will do it!" This is the attitude that you must adopt, but the good news is that this initial suffering does not last forever. In time, the suffering goes away.

When you start the task that you have been resisting, *feel* the pain. Really. *Feel* it! Then do it anyway for only 10 minutes. Rest 2 minutes. Go another 10 minutes. *(Don't forget to keep your tempo fast!)* Rest 2 minutes. Go another 10 minutes. Usually by the 3rd set of 10 reps (reps = minutes), you will be in flow or momentum. Your procrastination will be gone.

Now select two important and valuable tasks you have been procrastinating (like doing your taxes, paying a parking ticket, renewing your car insurance or finishing an office report). Take two tasks and each day for the next 30 days, do the routine of "3 sets of 10 reps". When you complete your first two tasks, start the next two on your list of to do things. Keep going like this daily for 30 days. After you have successfully completely 30 straight days of "procrastination-busting" using this technique, go another 30 straight days when another set of to-do items that you have been procrastinating. You will be well on your way to mastering the problem of procrastination–forever. Did you hear what I said? You will have mastered the problem of procrastination forever. You will be successful at setting and achieving your goals.

"The only things you regret are the things you didn't do."–Michael Curtiz

Step 3: Visualize Yourself Doing the Task Easily

Visualization in itself is a very important practice that should be done on a daily basis. We will talk at length about the power and practice of visualization in a later chapter on techniques of creative thinking. For now, let me show you how the practice of visualization will apply to the conquest of procrastination.

Set aside 10 to 15 minutes to be alone. Unplug the telephone. Sit down in a straight backed chair in a room where you will not be disturbed. Put your hands gently on your lap. Close your eyes and imagine a white movie screen about 10 feet in front of you. Have this movie screen cover your entire visual field. Breathe deeply. In through your nose and out throw your mouth in long deep breaths. Relax. Let your muscles relax from head to toe. Release all tension. Relax.

Once you feel that you have relaxed sufficiently and have a clear enough picture of the movie screen, begin to see yourself successfully going about doing the procrastinated task. In your imagination, you are *enjoying* the accomplishment of the task. You *see* yourself doing everything easily and efficiently. Visualize, see and feel the satisfaction and the joy of the task completed. Now slowly open your eyes, and go about doing what you just rehearsed in your mind. You should find that your resistence to begin has been reduced by about 50%.

Step 4: Create and Carry Around a Goal Card

If you own a computer, and who doesn't nowadays, open up the template part of a popular program such as Microsoft Word and look for a business card template. You then type in the description of your various to-be-accomplished goals on this business card. You print some out and carry them around with you in your wallet. Take out the card that contains the task that you want to accomplish, and read it out loud once in the morning and once before you go to bed, and always just before you *begin* the task. This is what a "procrastination busting business card" might look like.

"Action is eloquence."–
William Shakespeare

Goal: To Budget My Expenses

Starting now and by Friday of next week, I will have organized and completed my written budget of income and expenses for the purpose of getting out of debt and becoming financially free.

Figure 6 This is a Goal Card business card size that you carry around with you in your wallet to read out loud during certain times of the day.

With every reading of this business card, you will be ingraining the importance and the necessity of this task into your subconscious and "superconscious" mind. Doing this will make it easier and more likely to happen with little or no struggle.

Step 5: Write Down a To-Do List the Night Before

Are you a "list-person"? Well, if not, now is the time to start. Buy just writing a to-do list before you go to bed, and reading it aloud 3 times, you will have done a lot for weakening procrastination the minute you wake up the next day. Your subconscious mind will have prepared and have gotten ready you all night as you slept and dreamed. I use a note pad put out by Mead®. It's their yellow Mini Legal Pad.

• THE 12 LAWS OF SUCCESS •

Figure 7 This is the Mead® yellow Mini Legal Pad which is great for making to-do lists and all types of carry-around notetaking.

"Well done is better than well said."–Benjamin Franklin

Writing lists down before you go to bed, *prepares* your mind and allows you not to miss anything important that you should do the next day.

Step 6: Repeat "Do It Now!" 10 Times Before the Task

Now it is time for you to "pump yourself up"! As you begin each task quickly and briskly, repeat outloud 10 times as you start, "Do it now!" "Do it now!" Do it now!" *Force* yourself to start, and continue in this way for 10 minutes not-stop, then rest 2 minutes. Begin again for 10 minutes, continuing to chant, "Do it now!" "Do it now!" Do it now!" Rest 2 minutes, and then continue once more for the third set of 10 minutes, as you chant out loud 10 times again, "Do it now!" "Do it now!" Do it now!" You will be amazed at how effective this is to get you in the mood for doing what you have to do.

Step 7: Create a "Reward System" after Each Task Done

Reward yourself with something that you find pleasant after each 3 sets of 10 reps of completed activity. This is called positive reinforcement. Possible treats for yourself could be:
- eating an ice cream cone
- a walk around the block
- flipping through a magazine that you purchased
- renting that DVD you promised yourself
- making a phone call to a friend

Step 8: Refuse to Make Excuses

Agree with yourself not to fall prey to any of your usual rationalizations for not doing the task. What are rationalizations? They are seemingly good reasons for unacceptable behavior. "I can't do my taxes right now because I have to call Brian and find out what time we are going to the movie tonight." You know what I mean.

Step 9: Begin with a Detailed Written Plan

The more difficult and complicated the task, the more likely you will want to postpone and procrastinate it due to the fear of overwhelm. A very easy way to handle any complicated plan is to create a very detailed blueprint or step-by-step written of strategy of many simple steps that can easily be done when you focus on little tasks. As you complete the simple tasks, the entire project loses its ominous quality.

Step 10: Eat an Elephant

The way to understand how a detailed written plan works is to know how to eat an elephant. What? You *don't* know how to eat an elephant?...It's, bite by bite. This "procrastination-busting" principle has also been called the Salami Method. No one would ever attempt to eat a whole huge roll of salami, but it becomes very palatable once we slice it and eat it slice by slice. Focus on the many easy steps, and eat your elephant–bite by bite.

"To think is easy. To act is difficult. To act as one thinks is the most difficult of all."–Johann von Goethe

Step 11: Start with the Most Difficult Task First

If you are going to eat an elephant, choose an elephant of a task to begin with. You will find that when you start with the most difficult task first, everything else you have to do on your list will be much easier to do.

Step 12: Make an *Appointment* with Yourself

The twelfth step in our "procrastination busting" program is to make an appointment with yourself. Start an important task at a specified time on a given day – and *keep* your appointment with yourself! One of the most important principles of success is integrity or keeping your word. You must learn to keep your word with everyone, and you should of course begin with yourself.

"You are not only who you are today but also who you choose to become tomorrow."–
Melvin Powers

CHAPTER 15

Techniques of Creative Thinking

Techniques of Creative Thinking is a chapter that could easily merit an entire book treatise, but there are certain basic principles and techniques that I can lay out for you that can give you a tremendous headstart in becoming a creative thinker and problem solver.

What is Genius?

Simply put, genius is learning how to use more of your mind and to use it in a special way. The special way is to produce creative ideas at will. It has been said by many noted experts in the field of psychology and brain physiology that most of us are using only 1/10 of our mental capacities with a vast 90% of our mental capabilities being left as vast unused fertile wasteland, something like going about our daily lives using only the little finger of the left hand while ignoring the combined griping power of the ten fingers of both hands.

In this chapter, I will show you how to use more of your mind and how to use it in a special way–to produce creative ideas at will.

Left Brain/Right Brain Thinking

One of the most important discoveries in recent years on the total functioning of the human brain is the understanding of left and right brain thinking. From an early age while at school all the way up to and through adulthood, we have been conditioned almost exclusively to employ left brain type of thinking versus *right* brain thinking. Let me elaborate. If you look at a human brain, you will notice that there is a big cleavage right down the middle, separating the brain into two hemispheres–a right hemisphere and a left hemisphere. Left brain thinking is logical and analytical while right brain thinking is *imaginative* and *creative*. The right brain is also most active when we sleep and dream. All throughout school in our most creative reveries, we were admonished to "wake up and stop daydreaming". But ironically, it is in this imaginative, daydreaming state that our greatest creative treasures can be found. The goal is not to ignore left brain logical thinking, but to integrate and utitilize the left and right brain hemisphere to allow *whole*-brain thinking–the 'stuff" of which *geniuses* are made.

"Imagination is more important than knowledge."–
Albert Einstein

Creative Thinking through Creative Visualization

Our purpose is to find the quickest and most efficient techniques for producing happy, peaceful, joyous, healthy and prospering ideas by learning how to tap into this infinite resource of our *right brain* hemisphere. The key to this is a technique called *creative visualization* which if you practice daily for at least 21 days, you will see a marked difference in your creative ability.

For fifteen minutes before you go to bed and fifteen minutes ater you wake in the morning, I want you to prop yourself up in the bed. Turn off the TV, radio and disconnect the telephone. Make it clear to your family that you are not to be disturbed during these most important 15 minutes.

Count backwards slowly from 25 to 1, relaxing your entire body. With each retrogressive count, you will relax more, and more, and more. You are to now visualize yourself in your office or some other room familiar to you, and imagine that you are standing in front of and talking with an expert, living or dead, who is an expert on your problem. For example, if you are an artist and you have a problem coming up with newer and more creative ideas, you could imagine yourself standing in the room with Michaelangelo, Leonardo da Vinci and Raphael. If you are in need of money-making ideas that would serve you to prosper more in your present circumstance, you could see yourself in the company of three billionaires, like Bill Gates, Oprah Winfrey and Bob Johnson. If you are having relationship or marital problems, you could see yourself in the room with, Dr. David Viscott, Dale Carnegie and Dr. Laura Schlessinger. You get the idea. Just make sure that you choose three experts that you admire and feel what it would be like to have your luminaries in the room with you.

Whomever you choose to be your imaginary "mental couselor", mentally see yourself greeting him or her, and see him or her responding in turn. This is the technique: Let us say that you have a new business idea that you are trying to develop, and you would like to know of the best way to go about and get started to license and franchise it. You would simple pose a question like, "Mr. Gates, what in your opinion, is the first thing that I should do in my present situation to get started licensing my idea?" Pay attention here for this is key. The first thought that pops into your mind is your imaginary counselor's answer. Have a Mead® mini legal pad in your hand along with a pencil as you will write what comes to you—*with your eyes closes*—while the idea and answer is still fresh in your mind. (With practice, you can learn to write on a small note pad. It make look a little scratchy, but you will usually be able to make it out.)

In the beginning,, it will feel as though you are "making these answers up". This is the right feeling. Three things you will find as you

"Vision is the art of seeing things invisible."–Jonathan Swift

practice this ostensibly silly technique:

1) These imaginary answers will come faster and better each time.

2) Ideas will pop into your head when you least expect it all throughout the day. (So always keep you Mead® mini legal note pad and a pen on hand in your pocket with you.)

3) When you practice this visualization just before you go to sleep, you will increasingly have and remember dreams that will give you rich and creative ideas. Be not surprised when you awake at 4:00 a.m. with your head pregnant with really great and creative ideas ready for execution.

"A fool sees not the same tree that a wise man sees." – William Blake

"You are not only who you are today but also who you choose to become tomorrow."–
Melvin Powers

CHAPTER 16

Creative Dreaming

I am really, really excited about the writing of this chapter as it is something that I have wanted to share with the world perhaps for the last 30 years. I have dreamt my way to success many, many times. I have received answers to problems, ideas for new businesses and even correct diagnosis for illnesses before they have become worst. There is a whole *world* of experience awaiting you when you open yourself to the world of your dreams.

Throughout this chapter, you will be re-acquainted with a dear friend who has been with you since the moment of your conception, throughout the prenatal stay in your mother's womb, at birth and all throughout your life–and will continue to be with you all of your days. "Who *is* this friend?" This friend is your dream mind–that metaphysical part of your higher self which unlocks for you the creative solutions to your most challenging problems, warns you of impending dangers and delights you with beautifully exciting adventures throughout the quiet of the night.

More Than "Just a Dream"

Hopefully no more will you say, "just a dream" for every dream ignored or not remembered is just like an important letter left unopened by a giving benefactor. These are letters that your higher, wiser self writes–in code–to your learning, evolving self.

Dreams have been a fascination to mankind all throughout history. The mystery of dreams lies buried in a treasure chest of strange symbols and colorful metaphors which will soon become no more than a *learnable* picture *language* that can be deciphered and interpreted with practice. To understand and follow the guidance and help of your dreams is to truly avail yourself of the sweet whispers of the divine voice of God.

I would like to share with you right now one of the many, many creative experiences that I have had in dreams. One of the most charming and notable ones was when I was in my last year in college, I was very much into poetry. Not understanding the austere, *no-money in-their-pocket* life of a poet, for a brief spell, I wanted to be a famous poet. During this particular day, I had met a very attractive young lady

"Thou driftest gently down the tides of sleep."–Henry Wadsworth Longfellow

who absolutely fascinated me with her beautiful unforgettable eyes. After that day, I never saw her again, but I went to bed thinking about those eyes...those eyes...In a dream, I saw written across a blue sky, in this white sky writing much like that done by airplanes that specialize in writing messages across the sky. There. Up in the sky. Was a bird. No. A plane. No. It was a completed poem written out for me. I woke. Being accustomed to keeping a note pad and pen next to my bed, I wrote down everything that I could remember of the dream poem before it dissipated. For what it is worth, here is the dream poem:

Unforgettable Eyes

Soft
as the downy
ride
of lotuses
on a stream—

Gentle
as the
tender arms
that hold you
in a dream—

Playful
as the
drops of dew
rolling
down a flower—

Lovely
as the
falling stars
turning
to a shower—

Lovely fireflies
lost in Paradise—
Those are yours.

Unforgettable eyes.

Well, what would you expect from a 19-year old?

> *"Sleep is the most blessed and blessing of all natural graces."* –Aldous Huxley

Why You Dream

You dream quite simply to learn, to survive and to thrive. It is life's built-in guidance and protective system that allows you daily access to the deeper, wiser and more creative aspect of yourself. It is quite ironic how so many people run around in frantic circles, seeking out advice and help form the most unlikely sources when wise nightly counsel is available every time you close your eyes to sleep.

Our dreams allow us to look at our true feelings unfettered by our daily self-imposed prisons of denial. Once we truly understand the problem, it then becomes difficult to ignore. Like a true and loyal friend, these important messages will return again and again, in stronger and stronger images until ultimately they are heeded.

Dreams allow you to explore the most creative aspects of yourself. All of you who think you are not creative, say your dreams otherwise. Do you know that *your* dreams are just as rich and creative as the dreams of an Einstein, Bach, Edison, Washington Carver or Gary Larson? When we dream, we all share the collective (nightly) pool of genius. Genius, again, is simply defined as using more of your mind and using it in a very special way.

Dreams, particularly *lucid dreams*, which we cover later in this chapter, can lead you to incredible worlds of beauty, color and sensual delight, sometimes like our own personal built-in virtual reality system, our "holodeck", more life-like and breathtaking than any technological attraction of the modern world.

"It i a common experience that a problem difficult at night is resolved in the morning after the committee of sleep has worked on it."–John Steinbeck

An Owner's Manual

Have you ever bought a stereo system? When you do, it comes with an owner's manual of how to operate it, doesn't it? What about an auto? A DVD player? A refrigerator? A computer? These all come with the proper operating instructions, some sort of a handbook to follow is available. Life being no less wiser than man has also, through dreams, provided us with our own personal nighttime owner/operations "manual".

Who Dreams?

Whether you *remember* your dreams or not, it has been scientifically proven that we all dream, *every* night–in fact, *several* times during the night. Adults dream. Infants dream. It is believed that even dogs and cats dream as well as other animals. An interesting way which tells an outside observer when a person asleep is dreaming was discovered one day in a sleep study laboratory. About 90 minutes after a person has fallen asleep, it was observed that the eyeballs began to move rapidly back and forth under closed eyelids. This nightly phenomenon is called rapid-eye-movement or simple REM for short. It has been proven time and time again that when a subject is awakened during this activity, he or she accurately and vividly reports a dream that was taking place. The first period of REM lasts for 3 or 4 minutes before it gradually comes to a stop. Then every interval all throughout the night of 90 minutes, there are from 4 to 5 dream periods, each one progressively lasting longer and longer until the last dream period may last as long as an hour; this the one we usually remember upon awakening.

The Electroencephalograph (The EEG)

Another scientific way which determines when we are about to enter a dream time period is by means of a scientific device called an electroencephalograph or simply EEG for short. This is the machine which measures pulsations or brain wave activity in something scientists call cycles-per-second or cps. Througout the duration of the 6 to 8 hour sleep time for most people, the brain wave activity pulsates at certain speeds during 4 distinct stages of sleep. These 4 stages of sleep, each with a different rate of cps are respectively called: Beta, Alpha, Theta and Delta. Let us examine each of these 4 sleep stages in detail:

"O bed! O bed! Delicious bed! That heaven on earth to the weary head!"–Thomas Hood

1) **BETA** is the state of the fastest or most active brain rhythms. As you read these words, you are now in a Beta brain wave activity state. This brain wave activity is clocked at 20 to 13 beats per second. These pulsations are measured by an ink-filled needle which squiggles a line back and forth on top of a slow moving paper drum which receives the nerve transsions sent from wires which are taped to the forehead and scalp that are hooked into the EEG machine. When we go bed and begin to fall asleep, we are falling asleep from the Beta state. Within minutes of closing our eyes, depending on how fast or slow we fall asleep, our brain waves or cps begin to slow down from 20 to 15 to 13, and then we move into the *next* sleep stage called Alpha, which *starts* at 12 cycles per second.

2) **ALPHA** rhythms mark the beginning of REM activity (rapid-eye-movement) which is associated with the commencement of dream time. The first dream period lasts about 3 or 4 minutes. Alpha rhythms start at 12 cycles per second and eventually slow down to 8 cycles per second. Rapid-eye-movement soon begins to slow down, then stops as it approaches Theta, the next stage of sleep.

3) **THETA** begins at 7 beats per second. Theta is the state of deep sleep where there is no *observable* dream activity. This

brain wave measurement starts at 7 cps and slows down to 5 cps. The EEG needle slowly moves up and down like a rhythmic roller-coaster ride on a warm, sunny day.

4) **DELTA** is the final sleep phase which slows down even more. At a rhythm of 4 cycles per second, Delta is considered the stage of very deep sleep. There is still no observable dream activity. It is believed by some scientists that the body repairs and renews itself at this stage. By now, 90 minutes have passed. At 4 cycles per second, the brain activity gradually speeds up *again* to 12 cycles per second. REM activity starts anew, and we find ourselves again in Alpha time, dreaming another dream.

Each succeeding dream period of the Alpha state (the dream state) will be increasingly longer in duration than the previous Alpha period 90 minutes earlier.

Some Famous Dreams

All throughout history, some very famous people have had some very famous dreams, dreams that have in some important way enhanced or improved the quality of life for humanity.

Guiseppe Tartini, the famous 18th century Italian violinist and composer had a dream in his early career in which he sold his soul to the Devil. In this dream, he handed his fiddle to the Devil, who then played a sonata of incredible breathtaking quality. Upon awakening, he feverishly wrote down all of the sound and melody that he could recall. This dream led him to write one of his most creative musical masterpieces– *Trillo del Diavolo* or *The Devil's Trill*.

In the late 19th century, the German chemist, Friederich A. Keklule, revolutionized modern chemistry upon receiving an answer to a problem he had been arduously working on for many years. He was trying to discover the molecular structure of benzene, a clear, flammable, poisonous liquid used as a solvent in plastics and other materials today. In a dream, he saw a snake grab its own tail and form a circle which then began to twirl mockingly in front of his eyes. He then awoke to realize that the structure of benzene is a *closed carbon ring*.

Robert Louis Stevenson, the noted 19th century British author, developed the ability to request creative help for complete story ideas, while he slept, from his "dream friends," whom he fondly called his Brownies. Remarkably in a dream state, he would "dream up" entire story lines complete with characters, scenery and plot by simply requesting help before falling asleep. One of his most famous tales, which arose from one of his dream requests was *The Strange Case of Dr. Jekyll and Mr. Hyde.*

"Hold fast to dreams for if dreams die, life is a broken-winged bird that cannot fly." –Langston Hughes

The prolific inventor of the light bulb and phonograph, Thomas Alva Edison, is well-known for his "cat naps"; these he took around the clock, all throughout the day; many believe this to have been the fount of his inexhaustible creative ability, an ability which he apparently accessed through sleep and dreams.

Were I to list all of the guidance, help and inspiration that have taken place because of dreams, I could easily fill an endless tome of recorded accounts.

How to Remember Your Dreams

As we saw in the last chapter, everybody dreams, every night, several times a night, whether he or she remembers it or not. Why do some people easily remember their dreams and others almost never do? There are several reasons for either remembering or forgetting dreams, but it basically breaks down into three main categories:

1) culture
2) motivation
3) habit

"Every problem contains the seeds of its own solution."–
Stanley Arnold

Culture is probably *the* singularly most important element to natural dream recall. Certain cultures particularly encourage, value and revere their nightly dream messages. The indigenous Senoi tribe of the mountainous jungles of Malaysia is classic example of a culture whereupon the day is started with a discussion of the content of their dreams. From childhood all throughout adulthood, their dream life is a central theme of importance. The result is a very prolific dream recall among its members, young and old. Our native American Indian tribes such as: the Iroquois, the Ojibwa, the Cherokee, the Cheyenne and the Navajo, and others, all share the same reverence for dream revelations; a high level of dream recall always results. Ancient Greek and Egyptian cultures placed dream life in the center of their daily plans, resulting in a much higher overall incidence of dream recall than most members of modern Western civilization.

The influence of culture can be observed to some degree in an apparent difference of dream recall between males and females in our society. It is reported in some studies that women seem to have an overall higher incidence of dream recall than men in Western society. This observation has certainly been coroborated by all of the women in *my* life. My 13-year old daughter has always been a prolific dream recaller. At 8 years old, she told me of a man in her dream that had taken her vocal cords and had placed them on a table. In the dream, she has to go to school and use sign language all day. I asked her whom, in real life, did the man in the dream who took her vocal cords remind her. She said, "I think he reminded me of you." I immediately understood.

Recently, I had developed the nasty habit of interrupting her when I was instructing her to do something that she had omitted. I understood that this dream was telling her that I made her feel that I was taking away her right to express herself. I immediately explained to her the meaning. I sincerely apologize for this error. I promised that I would be careful not to do it again. She gave me a hug and a kiss. "It's okay, daddy, I still love you." Can you see how important dream discussion can be with your family?

Men as a rule are encouraged to be hard-nose, rational and logical whereas for women, generally speaking, it is much more permissable to be intuitive and imaginative.

Motivation is the Key to Dream Recall

You must be *committed* to your dream recall, dream interpreting, and dream recording as you would be committed to anything else in order to be outstanding and successful. This is a law. Motivation (or lack of it) enhances or decreases dream recall. By simply *wanting* to remember more of your dreams, you *automatically* begin to recall them. It has been noted by some dream researchers that a person who is desirous and intends to receive and recall the solution to a problem in dreams will have, during this period, almost 4 times his or her normal dream recall. Dreams have almost a childlike quality in that the more attention you give them, the more they will perform for you in cute, marvelous and surprising ways. Conversely, the more you ignore them, the more withdrawn and depressed they become.

Habit is linked, to some degree, to motivation. How you *start* your day upon awakening as a regular habit will determine the frequency and regularity of your dream recall. You must first of all go to bed *early*, enough to allow for a well-rested night and enough time to remember the night's dreams before you get up and rush off to work. Jumping out of bed the minute you wake up is definitely *not* conducive to remembering your dreams. *Taking your time* to think "What was I just dreaming?" most definitely is.

Programming Yourself to Remember Your Dreams

As a result of the electronic age, we have gotten used to a new parlance of speech as part of our computer explosion. We use the word *programming* to denote some type of operational command. There is a technique of autosuggestion whereby we can program our dream mind to perform certain tasks for us. It is a simple and effective procedure.

Wait about 30 minutes before the usual time you go to sleep and find a quiet room where you can be alone and undisturbed. Sit in a comfortable straight-backed chair, preferably without arms. Place your

"God doesn't make orange juice. God makes oranges." –Jesse Jackson

feet flat on the floor and your hands on your lap, palms facing up. Gently close your eyes, and take three very slow and deep breaths. You breathe in through your nose for a count of ten, hold your breath for a count of ten, and slowly exhale for another count of ten. You then repeat this process two more times of in-ten, hold-ten, and exhale-ten. Try to relax the muscles of your body, from head to toe, as much as possible. Mentally estimate ten to fifteen minutes of time and then silently repeat to yourself over and over—*with feeling*—"When I dream tonight, I will remember my dreams, *and* I will understand them upon awakening." The second part of this mental affirmation, "...and I will understand them..." is a very important element for learning to *interpret* your dreams and to be able to decode its special pictorial language.

Your Morning Dream Recall Ritual

To become an automatic and natural dream recaller, you must establish what I call Your Morning Dream Recall Ritual, which is broken down into seven steps:

1) Don't move.

2) Recall your dream.

3) Record dream on pad (eyes closed).

4) *Gently* roll over; record more.

5) Get up.

6) Tell your partner.

7) Record dreams in your journal.

Upon awakening from a dream, *don't move!* That's right. Don't move your bodily position *at all*, even if you've been sleeping on your arm all night and you suddenly feel like stretching it. Any quick or jerky bodily movement will tend to interrupt and fragment any fresh dream images. If you resist this temptation to move and turn, you will find that surprisingly you'll be able to recall images and thoughts you believed were lost. *In reverse order,* you will recall entire dream scenes starting with the dream you were having upon awakening—then the one before that—and then the one before that.

Your initial dream recall should always be done with *eyes closed* and before you begin to start to think about any other activity of the day. A little later in this chapter, I will detail the specific way for you to

> *"We are the wire, God is the current. Our only power is to let the current pass through us."*—Carlo Carretto

record your dreams with your eyes still closed on your 3" x 5" mini legal note pad.

After you have recalled all of your dream stories you can on this note pad, gently roll over to another sleep position and record more. For some unknown reason, by simply rolling over to another sleep position, you will oftentimes recall additional dreams of the night. If you are not getting any more new dream images as you gently roll over to your different sleep positions, it helps to think about the persons in your life one by one. This may trigger an association with a certain dream you had that night and thus more dream recall.

After practicing this routine for a couple of weeks, don't be surprised if you find yourself waking up spontaneously in the middle of the night after a dream. Don't become alarmed or feel that this is the onset of some strange sleep disorder. Your dream mind is responding to your wishes to recall more dreams, and so you may begin to occasionally wake after a dream cycle. Simply record your dream on your note pad, with eyes still closed and fall back to sleep. Paradoxically, each time you wake up and fall back asleep, your sleep becomes more and more refreshing.

"Belief is the only door through which the power of God can flow."–Charles Prosper

Once your have recorded your last dream upon awakening in the morning, you get up and start your daily routine. If you are lucky enough to have loving companion with whom you share your life, my next advice would be to share your dreams with your partner on a regular basis. (This can be especially helpful on those days when it is just not possible to take the time to write them down.) If your partner is also interested in dreams, he or she can help you interpret them. (If you don't have a partner, you can share your dreams later on in the day with a close friend or relative.)

The final step of your morning dream recall ritual is to make a permanent, formal record in a special dream journal. We'll cover in detail later on in this chapter on how to keep a dream journal. One more thing, don't become surprised when you recall a dream suddenly in the middle of the day in an unexpected flash triggered by something you see or something someone says. Whenever this happens, jot it down *immediately*, and record it later in your dream journal. Above all, remember that no matter how weird, strange or funny the dream image may be, there is no such thing as an unimportant dream image. All dreams have *some* message to convey. *All* dreams bring gifts and secrets. Our task is to find the key to open the magic box.

How to Keep a Dream Journal

One of the most important decisions to unlocking the treasures and gifts of your dreams is how to record and organize your dream life. Your dream journal will become an important and priceless chronicle of life issues and how your were guided to solve them.

The first step to chronicle and understand your dreams is to properly select your recording tools. These are:

1) Your yellow mini legal pad which measures 3" x 5" and can fix in the palm of the hand, Figure 7, page 112

2) A medium-point, black ball-point pen that clicks in and out from the top with a flick of the thumb

3) A spiral notebook which measures about 6.75"wide x 9.5" high, Figure 4, page 92

I recommend that you use the same color and style spiral notebook for uniformity sake and for aesthetics. On the cover of each notebook with a thin permanent marker, you can write Dream Diary Volume 1 (or 2, or 3, or 4, etc.) and the year. If you finish a complete volume within a few months, then go back and write on the cover from what-month-to what-month before you start your next volume.

"To believe with certainty, we must begin without doubting."–Charles Prosper

How to Record Your Dreams with Your Eyes Closed

To be able to first record your dreams upon awakening with your eyes still closed, you'll need to know how to do this on your mini legal note pad. (Your note pad is placed at your bedside each night along with your ballpoint pen.) Assuming you write with your right hand, hold the pad vertically in your left hand. If you are left-handed, simply reverse the instructions. After you have mentally recalled all of your dream images, begin to write on this pad by placing your thumb and middle finger on the upper left and right edges respectively of both sides of the pad, holding the rest of it in the lap of your palm. (The description sounds much more complicated than it really is. Once you begin to attempt to do it, you immediately will understand the procedure.) Your thumb and middle finger position serve as a point of reference as you write with your eyes closed moving horizontally, left to right across the pad. After finishing a line of description, you then simultaneously slide these two "guide-fingers" down the sides of the pad a half inch or so, as you begin to write another line at the new position of the thumb, a half inch lower than the line above. In the same way that the carriage of an old-fashioned typewriter moved left to right, then down a line and continues left to right again; this is the way you're writing also. As you write, to keep as straight as possible, extend the index finger of your writing hand and touch the middle finger of the bracing hand. Write evenly and carefully. Though there will be *some* wobbly words when you read it later, you should be able to read it nonetheless. (And don't become too concerned about crossing t's and dotting i's. Remember, your eyes are closed. You don't get a grade for penmanship.)

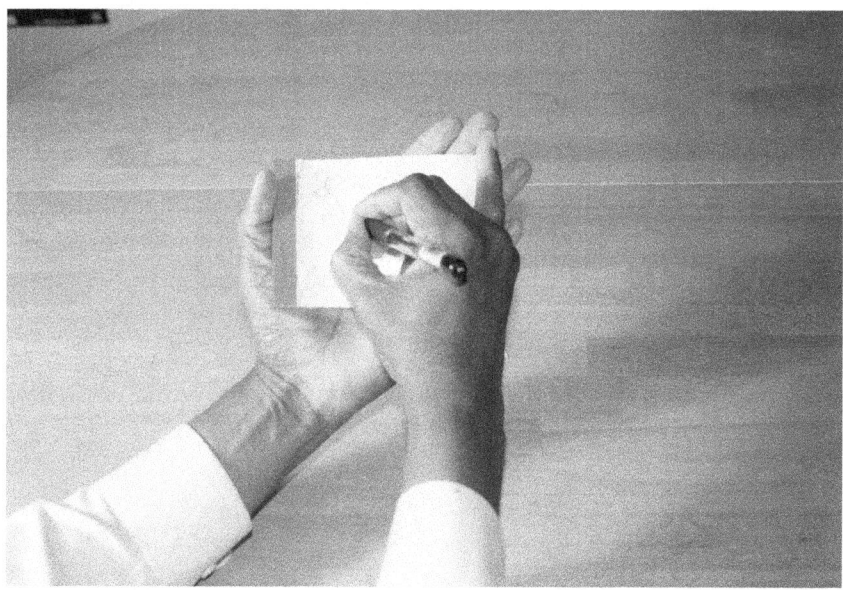

Figure 8 This is proper way to hold your dream note pad as you record your dreams upon awakening with your eyes closed.

"What you can do, or dream you can do, begin it; boldness has genius, power and magic in it."–Johann von Goethe

When you finish jotting down all of your dream, write the word **Feeling**, followed by a hyphen and them in a few words describe the dominant feeling of the dream. You would write: happy, sad, confused, worried, confident, etc. after the Feeling. Many times as you *write* a dream, you intuitively *know* the meaning. When you suddenly sense the meaning as well, write down the word **Meaning**, also followed by a hyphen. Then write a very brief description of the dream's meaning. After this is done, write down the date underneath the entire record as in 4/23, 10/2 or 11/3. (You need not write down the year at this time. Draw a straight line under the date to indicate the ending of a dream before another one starts.) You then fall back to sleep and continue to dream more.

The Key Elements of a Dream Journal

When you are ready to make a formal entry into your spiral dream notebook, there are several key elements to outline in every journal entry. These are:

1) Date

2) Journal

3) Dream Request (optional)

4) Title

5) Dream

6) Feeling

7) Outstanding Symbol

8) Background

9) Theme

10) Meaning

11) Summary

12) Plan of Action

"Our remedies oft in ourselves do lie."–William *Shakespeare*

The best way to illustrate how these key elements work is to give you an example of a dream journal entry as you'd see it in your spiral notebook.

December 7, 2004

JOURNAL - I am contemplating quitting my present job tomorrow without giving prior notice in order to take advantage of an unexpected job offer which promises better pay and greater benefits, even though my quitting would upset the operations of my department and would justifiably anger my employer.

DREAM REQUEST - "Should I accept this new job offer right away, or should I give my present employer a 2-week notice to find my replacement?" (You then go to bed after writing in your dream request.)

December 8, 2004

TITLE - (To be decided and written after you've written down your dream and have analyzed and interpreted it by means of the following steps, in particular the summary.)

DREAM - I am running down the hallway of present employer screaming in pain with the seat of my pants on fire. Scorching orange flames sear my tail as they leave a trail of thick, black smoke following behind me wherever I go. I wake.

FEELING - Panic and regret.

OUTSTANDING SYMBOL - Burning trousers.

BACKGROUND - My present place of employment.

THEME - I am trying to undue a bad situation.

MEANING - The primary image of this dream is the pain of the burn-pants (or breeches). The colloquial substitute for *breeches* (which refers to any trousers) are *britches*. So now we have "*britches* burning behind me" which is an audible play on words for "*Bridges* burning behind me." The meaning and message now becomes clear. The answer to my dream request is: "Don't burn *bridges* behind you!" In other words, don't abruptly quit your present job without giving your employer the consideration of a two-week notice because you might need them again later.

SUMMARY - I would be making a mistake to quit my present job without giving notice first.

PLAN OF ACTION - Explain to my prospective new employer that it would be necessary to give my present employer a two-week notice before I could begin.

"We will either find a way, or make one." –Hannibal

After finishing the Plan of Action, you would then write in a title for this dream at the above section marked TITLE. The title for our sample dream here could be **Burning Bridges**.

Your JOURNAL entry which is your first key element is always a synopsis of the day's key events and issues that you are currently facing. The date above your journal entry is the date you make this entry which will usually be just before you go to bed.

The date that is written just about the TITLE of your dream is the date of the _morning_ of the dream.

Your Weekly Dream Review

Though you have as many as five dream periods throughout each night, my recommendation is that you do whatever it takes to properly record, journal and interpret at least *one* dream per day. You will be greatly rewarded with the insights and guidance you need which will result from this daily discipline. Later this practice will become a way of life and a joyous and precious habit which you will forever appreciate and cherish.

Assuming that you have recorded and journaled at least one dream per night for seven consecutive nights on a regular basis, you should do a *weekly review* of your dreams. This is done by reading over all of the week's dreams, paying very close attention to recurrent themes and consistent advice.

Your Monthy Dream Review

Your monthly dream review is started on the page after you record your last dream of the month. On the top of this page, you write *Monthly Dream Review*. Leave about six blank lines under the monthly dream review heading so that later you'll have enough space to write in your *Monthly Dream Theme Summary*. On about the seventh line from the top, begin a summary of every dream you have had in the month of July 2007, or whatever the month and year happen to be.

This is how your Monthly Dream Review entries for the month might look:

> TITLE: **Sweet Romantic Night**   7/1/07
> SUMMARY: I should expect a beautiful and positive change soon.
>
> TITLE: **My Personal Trainer**   7/2/07
> SUMMARY: God is with me, supporting me, helper me become stronger through problems (weights).
>
> TITLE: **Teaching a 2-Year Old**   7/3/07
> SUMMARY: I must go back to basics and do what I love and let the money flow.
>
> TITLE: **Pressing the Computer Keys**
> 7/4/07
> SUMMARY: I must press (activate) the keys to my success which is to take action and do whatever it takes.

This Title-Summary combination with the date to the right will continue until every dream for the month has been entered. After all of the month's dreams have been entered in this way, go back up to the top of the page right under the heading of *Monthly Dream Review*. Skip a line then write in the the heading *Monthly Dream Theme Summary for July 2007*. Go to the next line and write *Monthly Title* and then to the next

"I finally figured out the only reason to be alive is to enjoy it." –Rita Mae Brown

Your Monthly Dream Review

Monthly Dream Theme Summary for July 2007
Monthly Title: Pursuing Your Purpose
Monthly Summary: Trust God. Do what you love and expect success.

Your monthly title and your monthly summary gives you the *essence* of the month's message and guidance.

Your Yearly Summary

Your Yearly Summary begins after you have finished the Monthly Dream Review for December. Your Yearly Summary is done by writing down each of the twelve monthly summaries. An example of how this would look is as follows:

January Dream Summary (2007)
Monthly Title: Letting Go of the Past
Monthly Summary: Do not hold on to that which no longer servers you.

February Dream Summary (2007)
Monthly Title: Look Within for Help
Monthly Summary: Begin a daily practice of prayer and meditation.

March Dream Summary (2007)
Monthly Title: Prosperity Awaits You
Monthly Summary: Do what you love and the money will follow.

This is continued for each month until you finish with the month of December.

The final phase of your end-of-year dream review is to write down the Title and the Message for the *entire* year, for example:

2007 Yearly Summary
Yearly Title: Be True to Yourself
Yearly Summary: If you trust God, yourself and take action with courage, you will succeed.

Your Yearly Summary, which is good to do no later than the morning of December 31st, is the basis for the setting of your New Year's resolutions.

"Results are what you expect; consequences are what you get." –Anonymous

There is one more bit of advice on keeping an effective dream journal and that is to be careful that you not let too many unjournaled dreams accumulate on your mini legal note pad. One of the ugliest feelings is to have mastered good dream recall and to have four, five or more days of dreams on your bedside note pad but unrecorded in your journal. New dreams are coming in daily that also require attention and to be recorded. So rather than allow yourself to become overwhelmed and to eventually fall out of your discipline of organized dream study, I would suggest that you read over all of the unrecorded dreams that you have on your note pad and interpret their important messages, then *throw* it all away and start again frest the next morning. It is of course better to never get behind, but it we were perfect or not human, we wouldn't ever need guidance from dreams or any thing else, would we?

This type of record-keeping requires some commitment, discipline and organization at first, but within a few days or weeks, it becomes fun, and the result is only a quality of life and enjoyment that only gets better, better and better.

How to Learn to Interpret Your Dreams

"I had a weird dream last night." "Dreams are no more than random nerve discharges of the day's events." "My dreams are always too silly to bother with." I am sure that you have either heard or said one or more of these statements at one time or another; they all reflect the frustration of not being able to understand a dream's meaning immediately. When something doesn't make sense or is confusing, there is a tendency to ignore it, discard it or simple claim that it's not important. Everything *means* something. A *meaning* implies a *connection* to *something else*, and that something else is connected to still something else and so on and so forth, until the ultimate source of All-That-Is is touched. Just because a meaning is not immediately apparent does not mean that one does not exist. A person who has never experienced Russian or any other foreign language could falsely conclude that because he or she does not understand what is uttered that no meaning could possibly exist. In calling a dream silly, weird or absurd without accepting that it is a distinct and unique *language* is to forfeit the magical gift of its message.

Dream Dictionaries

When someone thinks of dream interpretation, one of the first thing that comes to mind are dream dictionaries. This is the easiest and the most *obvious* route to interpret a dream because so many of them are available, but dream dictionaries are not necessary the most accurate route. Dream images and symbols have such a unique and *personal* meaning for each individual that no dream dictionary could accurately

"We pray to God that He may answer our prayer, and God prays to us that we may believe–so that we may receive that which we pray for."–Charles Prosper

portray *exactly* what's going on in everyone's life at any given time. Even what a symbol or image means to you *now* will oftentimes change completely from one period of your life to another. A common example of this might be the dream image of your *mother* or a *bicycle*. A dream of your mother during *childhood* might mean that this dream is communicating a message of care and nuturing. A dream of your mother during *adolescence* might symbolize restrictions and discipline. And a dream of your mother in *adulthood* might signify her need to be cared for. Likewise, *bicycle* at childhood might mean fun and adventure, at adolescence a traffic accident and in adulthood comptetion or racing. So as you can see, the meaning of dream symbols vary from person to person and even from one life period to the next. This does not however, mean that dream dictionaries are useless. Dream dictionaries *can* be very useful if one understands its limitations. A dream dictionary should be used to *stimulate* your imagination into thinking of *possible* meanings that feel right and fit your current situation. Dream dictionaries are a good *start*, but the rule of thumb is that the meaning offered must "feel right" *and not be forced*. You will always have an intuitive "knowing" when you have the "right" meaning.

Of all of the dream dictionaries and books on the market, the one that I highly recommend for the beginning dream explorer is *The Mystical Marvelous World of Dreams* by Wilda B. Tanner published by Sparrow Hawk Press of Tahlequah, Oklahoma. This book can be found at Amazon.com and at most major bookstores, and I classify it as must-reading.

"The purpose of life is a life of purpose."–Robert Byrne

Create Your Own Dream Glossary

Once you have some reasonable experience in interpreting the unique meanings of your personal dream symbols, you can eventually create your own dream dictionary (or glossary) of any recurrent dream images and place it starting at the last fifty pages or so of your spiral dream diary.

What's Going On In Your Life?

The key to understanding the meaning of your dreams is to understand what's going on in your life at present. Dreams typically comment, instruct, guide and give messages on those issues concerning your current needs and current life experiences. This is why the very first part of your formal dream journal is an entry of your daily record of the day's *key* events and any issues that you happen to be dealing with. A daily journal regularly kept as the first part of your overall Dream Journal serves not only as a diary of your life but also as a way to gauge your personal and spiritual evolution as you respond to and alter your actions in accord with the wisdom, guidance and insights of your higher self within your dream world.

The *Picture* Language of Dreams

To approach dream interpretation in the simplest way possible and to demystify any preconceived notions of its esoteric ineffability is to understand once and for all that we are simply dealing with a new *language*. The essence of all language is in the use of a *substitute*, be it visual auditory or tactile to *represent* or stand in the place of an idea. Language is *not* the idea. The idea is ethereal and doesn't have any *material* existence, yet nonetheless *does* exist as evidenced by the fact that we see its *effect* in the "material" world. Another way to call this *substitute* which *carries* language is to call it a symbol. Quite literally language is a system of symbols used for the purpose of carrying an idea (or many ideas) from one mind to another. When a language is *visual*, it could be something like the ancient Egyptian hieroglyphics which were elaborate paintings and pictures used to communicate thoughts, events and information. When a language is *auditory*, it could be like the native African or Native American drum beats which uses sound and music to communicate its meaning. And when language is *tactile*, we can easily think of Braille, the system of touch which allows the blind to read with their fingertips.

All language is a system. All systems have basics. All basics never change. Once you understand the basics, you can move through the system and easily understand the language. The basis for understanding dream language lies withing the understanding that the dream basic is the visual *metaphor*.

What is a Metaphor?

To understand the language of metaphor is to understand the language of your dreams. What exactly is a metaphor? A metaphor is a *pictorial* means of communicating an idea. Even though you may not be familiar with the term metaphor, it is something that we use quite commonly in our daily lexicon. "All the world is a stage." "It's raining cats and dogs." "She is the apple of my eye."

Pictures convey meaning much more economically and powerfully than words. Have you ever heard that one picture is *worth a thousand words?* No matter what means of language that we use: visual, auditory or tactile, the ultimate aim, wittingly or not, is to create a mental *picture* in the mind of the recipient. The mind thinks, understands and communicates in mental *pictures* which trigger, evoke and/or create *feelings* deep within the being of the reader; poetry's most effective device of communication is the metaphor. *"Soft as the gentle ride of lotuses on a stream; gentle as the tender arms that hold you in a dream..."* so sayeth the poet. Prayer is also powerful in its spiritual effect upon an

"Faith is to believe what we do not see; the reward of this faith is to see what we believe." –Saint Augustine

individual because it too uses the *metaphor* to communicate its spiritual truths to the heart of he who prays. For example, "The Lord is my *shepherd*; I shall not want." It is curious and interesting to me how so many "new" psychotherapies pop up such as Psychosynthesis and Neuro-Linguistic Programming used by many psychiatrists today, whereby they have their patients visualize powerful and meaningful pictorial metaphors which have the effect of making positive changes in the belief system of the individual; certain poetry and certainly prayer have been doing these same things for centuries.

Knowing that all of the "strange" images of many dreams are but symbolic metaphors allows us to look at some practical steps as to how we might go about *decoding* these metaphors. Upon writing down your dreams into your permanent journal as accurately as possible, the first step is to underline the action verbs. Take a look at the following example of a dream that is taken from one of my dream entries:

<u>Crossing Over</u>

I am <u>crossing</u> a bridge with someone who needs my help to <u>arrive</u> on the campus of Xavier University. I find myself on top of a high ladder whereby I must carefully <u>descend</u>, step-by-step, back down to solid and safe ground.

"He who fears he shall suffer already suffers what he fears."–Michel de Montaigne

The action verbs in this dream: <u>crossing</u>, <u>arrive</u> and <u>descend</u> were very significant at the time I had this dream because it was during a life experience of an important transition I had to make of giving up a lucrative retail business to dedicate myself to writing and the formation of my personal development training which I have discovered and now accepted to be my life's mission.

After you have underlined the action verbs to glean a meaning, another basic procedure could be to put the *nouns* in a square around the words: *bridge, campus, ladder* and *ground*. You would then ask yourself, "When I think of a *bridge*, what ideas coome to mind?" In *my* case, it was a message to me about making a transition; this idea was also re-inforced by the verb *crossing*. *Campus* indicated further learning and teaching awaiting me. *Ladder* indicated a high and uncertain place where I was in life. And ground indicated humbleness and my "coming down to earth."

When you begin to closely study dreams, you will notice the volatile nature of visual images. Sometimes a symbol, a person or a thing, will instantly "morph" or change from one image to another, back and forth several times. A desk becomes a dog. Your mother becomes your boss. These instant dream changes indicate the shared characteristics and shared personalities that reflect some aspect of *your* multi-faceted personality.

Meaning is Multi-Layered

The beauty of the dream metaphor is that it is often like a many-leveled layer cake, that is, the deeper you go into it, the more layers you discover. (Notice my use of a metaphor, *cake*, to talk about the beauty of the metaphor itself. How interesting!) A dream of heart trouble could mean that you need to check your cholesterol *and* that an emotional problem may be brewing between you and your spouse. Some dream symbols are very profound and have many, many levels of meanings and associations.

Speak As Your Dream Symbol

After you have set up and gone through all of the mechanical procedures for your dream interpretation, such as writing down your dream in your journal, noting the outstanding symbol, underlining key action words and placing symbolic nouns in boxes.

I will now give you one of the most powerful and unfailing dream interpretation techniques available today. Quite simply and literally, you will *ask your dream symbol* as though it were a person. You must understand that each dream image is a personified message that is trying to reach out to you by visual means. "But how can I talk to a dream symbol?" you might ask. This is done *mentally* just before you have been roused to full waking consciousness. This method requires keen attention and right timing as you begin to awaken.

As you are waking up and recalling a particular dream scene, image, person or object, ask for example, "Step Ladder, who are you, and what are you trying to tell me?" or maybe, "Muhammad Ali" who are you, and what are you trying to tell me?" You will get a subtle, but distinct, *feeling-answer* almost before you can finish asking the question. The *first* answer you feel to your question is usually the right one, 99% of the time. It sometimes is not the answer you were *expecting*, and the answer you receive may come to you as a shock.

The "That's-Not-Good-Enough" Reaction

The pitfall to avoid is the "That's-not-good-enough reaction". This means that when you get an answer that you don't want to hear, the tendency is to discard the "bad" news, pretend it's not good enough and then proceed on an intellectual (versus an intuitive) level to "second guess" a meaning that is more "appealing." An illustration of this folly is once when I dreamt of myself driving down a one-way street against rush traffic endangering my life. While lying in bed, as I began to recall the entirety of this dream, I quickly and mentally asked myself "One-Way-Street, who are you, and what are trying to tell me?" The *immediate*

"Forgiveness is the sweetest revenge." –Isaac Friedmann

feeling-response was "Don't marry Rosa. You are putting your life in danger." "Wow!" I thought. I didn't want to hear *that*. I wanted a "better" answer. I didn't want to examine closer a person with whom I was to marry. Well, the good news is that I *heeded* the wisdom of this dream, saw things I didn't *want* to see, and I *saved* myself from what would have been a terrible mistake.

Speak to Your Dream Symbols in Seated Visualization

There is another way to speak mentally to and as your dream and this is through seated meditation and visualization. Though the subject of visualization and meditation requires a complete treatise in itself, I will attempt to encapsulate a simple procedure as it applies to dream interpretation. If you allow yourself to come to full wakefulness before you have a chance to question your dream symbols, you have a second chance in seated meditation. After you have gotten up, find a comfortable straight-backed chair, preferably without arms. Place your feet flat on the floor, your hands in your lap, and gently close your eyes. Take a deep breath in through your nose for the count of ten, holding it for a count of ten, and slowly exhale again for a count of ten.

See whatever symbol, object or dream person walk into a room where you are seated and sit itself in a chair directly in front of you. No matter how weird you think this symbol is, allow it to take a seat in front of you. Picture the dream image as clearly and lifelike as possible. Then ask, for example, "Rainbow Kite, who are you, and what are you trying to tell me?" The *first* impression, feeling, "guess" or response that you get is the answer. You may feel as though your are "making it up"; this is the right feeling. Trust it. As you do, your answers in the future will clearer, faster and stronger. Doubt destroys. Faith fosters.

Some Aspect of You

The key to understanding any image or dream symbol is that it is *always* describing some aspect of *you* in a picture language. That *"raging bull"* is describing some aspect of *you*. That *"flood in your home"* is describing some aspect of *your* experience. *"Groucho Marx"* joking around in your dream is describing some aspect of *your* humorous behavior or the way you are *viewing* a situation. Your dreams are *you* in picture form.

Recurrent Dreams

Sometimes we experience dreams that repeat themselves in theme and general content during different periods of our lives. Sometimes these repeated dreams span over the course of months, and even years. These dreams we call recurrent dreams. When you don't get the message the first time, the messenger, so to speak, comes again and again. There is

"We carry with us the wonders we seek without us." –Sir Thomas Browne

lesson that you need to learn or some action that you need to take. When you have a repeated dream, make no mistake about it, there is an important issue that you must deal with. Once you understand the message and make the correction, the recurrent dream will usually stop.

Nightmares

Nightmares are those dreams which can be extremely frightening or disturbing. It is a forceful attempt of the mind to get your attention to get across a message that can no longer be ignored. Horrific nightmares can result during the detox period of alcoholic withdrawal. also called *delirium tremens*. Alcohol which depresses the nervous system is also known to interfere with dreams. In the case of alcohol addiction, proper dream functioning has been suppressed and disturbed over such a long period of time that when the alcoholic attempts to cross back over to the threshold of normalcy, nightmares may indeed result.

Proper and regular dreaming, whether we remember them or not, has been proven in scientific dream laboratory experiments to be absolutely essential for the maintenance of the psychological and emotional well-being of the individual. Whenever dream subjects were deprived of their dream time (REM periods) by waking them up at the onset of rapid-eye-movement, but otherwise were allowed to sleep through the *non*-rapid-eye-movement (NREM) periods, were found to become after only a few short days of this treatment, nervous, anxious and paranoid. Many individuals began to have serious hallucinations during the day, and all indications conclude that if persisted, eventual psychosis and complete mental breakdown would ensue denying the time to dream. Dream deprivation studies conclude these "daytime nightmares" (an oxymoron) can occur in the normalcy of waking consciousness.

Occasional nightmares in the life of an otherwise normal individual may well indicate an unhealthy fascination with fear images and death as depicted in horror movies or horror novels. But more likely than not, it indicates the ignoring and/or suppression of some vital or life-saving messages.

Dreamlettes

Sometimes you may remember only a fragment, an image, a feeling or a very small part of a dream. This is called a dreamlette. You should place value on both complete dreams *and* partial dream gifts. Even one fragmental image has *some* meaning. There is oftentimes the tendency and the temptation not to even bother to *record* certains dreams because they are only fragments of a longer and unremembered dream. Because you don't have the slightest idea of what a certain image could mean, you may erroneously conclude that the *part* does not also contain the

"Don't ask of your friends what you yourself can do."–
Quintus Ennius

essence of the whole. Holistically speaking, the essence of the whole is always contained in each and every one of its *parts*. I could cite many examples of this in physics, biology or chemistry. A drop of water has all of the molecular components of the ocean from which that drop of water came. Any cell tissue taken from any part of the body has the same DNA genetic code of the total body organism. I say to you also, that if you have but a fragment of a dream, you also have within that fragment the essential meaning of the whole dream.

All dreamettes have meaning. All dreams, whole and part, have a message or would have never been dreamt. Your intellect (your ego mind) always demands immediate control and instant understanding and is ever ready to discard your unpolished and uncut jewels. The so-called silliest of dreams, later after deciphering their hidden messages, have some of the most profound and relevant meaning. Honor and record *all* of your dream gifts, even if it is just a fragment, a single image, a word, a phrase, or a feeling.

Form a Dream Study Group

Dream interpretation is enhanced and always made much more fun when you share your dream world with like-minded individuals. Dreams become easier to remember because many times a friend or relative will remember a dream that you shared with him or her one morning long after you have forgotten about it.

"Faith doesn't wait until it understands; in that case it wouldn't be faith." –Vance Havner

If you are fortunate enough to find and become a part of a dream study group that meets every couple of weeks or so, by all means do so. It can be one of the most enlightening and enriching experiences of your life. If you can't find one–*form one!* It need not be more than two or three people besides yourself. Each person brings one or two dreams to be interpreted with the help of the group, and conclusions and resolutions are made for each dream.

Creative Problem Solving

Once you understand how to remember your dreams, how to record them and how to interpret them, you are now ready to actively use them to help you to creatively solve any problem you might possibly face. All problems are no more than the absence of an idea. Within you lies an infinite fount of problem-solving potential. Once you know how to *creatively* solve problems, problem-solving becomes <u>fun</u>.

Your dream mind is *constantly* attempting to determine what are your most important life issues and *how* you might improve or control them. Our dream mind *delights* when we consciously go to it for guidance.

Ask Your Dreams for Help

"Seek, and ye shall find. Ask, and it shall be given unto you."– is to paraphrase a noted verse of scriptual wisdom. Asking is the key to the answer. As always, the greatest truths are the simplest. If you but only ask your dream mind for help, it *will give you the answer* that you need. Now the question is, "*How* do you ask for help?" The best and fastest way to program your dream mind for solutions is to pose a *problem-question* before you retire each night–*until you receive your answer*.

Wait about an hour before you normally go to bed and start to get sleepy. Sit in a comfortable straight-backed chair preferably without arms, your feet flat on the floor, hands in your lap, and your eyes closed. Take three deep breaths, inhaling through your nose for a mental count of ten, holding your breath for a mental count of ten and finally exhaling through your slightly opened mouth for another count of ten. This would complete your first cycle of breath which you would follow up with two more cycles just the same. You now pose a problem-question slowly and repeatedly with as much *feeling* as possible. Your question may be posed as such:

a) "What can I do to create the money this month to pay my rent?"

b) "Should I go through with this marriage, or should I postpone it?"

c) "What is the best choice to make concerning my decision about _____ ?"

These are only a few examples. You can form a limitless variety of problem questions.

The next step to assure a clear and precise answer later in the night is to *visualize* yourself in a dream and *imagine* you are conversing with whomever represents for you in waking life the expert on your subject. If you have a problem with money, you might imaging you are having a dream where you are talking with J. Paul Getty, Donald Trump or John D. Rockefeller. If your problem is on a relationship you need to resolve, you could see yourself dreaming that you are conversing with Dr. David Viscott or Dr. Albert Ellis or any famous relationship psychiatrist or psychologist that you admire. If your problem concerns getting new ideas for art, you might conjure up the image of Salvador Dali or Leonardo Da Vinci and see yourself in a dream asking them for creative artistic ideas. You need not to try to force an answer; you need only to mentally *ask* the question, see your expert moving his or her lips and giving you an answer. See yourself jumping for joy and feeling thankful for the answer. Imagine yourself waking up the next

"A consciousness of God releases the greatest power of all."–Science of Mind

morning with the perfect solution in mind.

When you answer comes, it may come in various ways. You may dream of an expert who indeed gives you the answer, or the dream may come with a different group of images, symbols or metaphors, but rest-assured, the answer *will* come. It is even quite possible that you will not remember any *details* of the dream at all, but rather you will wake up with just a *feeling*. All of a sudden, you might have an unexpected rush of ideas lasting sometimes a half an hour or more, just as you are getting out of bed. Dream answers may also come during the day in what we might be called, the "Aha!" experience. You must remember that once you set your mind into motion, it literally works non-stop twenty-four hours a day, until it comes up with your answer. So once you make a dream request, be readly at all times, even *all throughout the day* with your pen and mini note pad.

The total time to program a dream solution before retiring should be a minimum of fifteen minutes.

Allow 21 Days for Your Answer to Come

There is one other key to making your creative problem-solving through dreams effective. This is called persistent patience. When a dream solution is requested, you may very well not receive your answer on the first try, *or* you may *receive* it but not *recall* it. Therefore, you must repeat your dream request again and again *every* night, until you receive it. It will come. If you were to suddenly stop trying, it is highly unlikely that you would find your answers faster or better by any other means. What I am saying is that 99% of everyone who faithfully perfoms this dream request technique for at least 21 days without fail *will* receive the answer that they seek.

Acting on Your Dream Guidance

The universe rewards action. Creative solutions, right answers and the "Aha!" experience will do you absolutely no good until you *act* on the advice that you receive. The universe rewards action in that action *always* produces results. When you find your answer – *act on it!*

Lucid Dreaming–Know You're Dreaming *while* You're Dreaming

How would you like to experience the ultimate virtual reality each night free of charge while you sleep? How would you like to choose and have an intense, erotic encounter with the person of your choice, past, present or fictional, and be in complete conscious control of the experience? How would you like to visit distant planets of unprecedented beauty, where benevolent inhabitants welcome you to cities of crystal and light? Have a problem on the meaning of life? Talk it over with the Buddha amidst gardens of fragrant flowers and running brooks.

"You'll see it when you believe it."–Wayne Dyer

Want to start a business? Why not discuss it with Napoleon Hill (author of *Think and Grow Rich*)? Are you over fifty and want to start an exercise program? Why not let the youthful 92 year old fitness guru, Jack LaLanne, take you through your first workout? In a lucid dream state, you may even visit the realms of heaven, talk with angels and touch the face of God. Sensual experience, inner peace, financial freedom, eternal health, spiritual enlightenment—the infinite spectrum of all conceivable human experience are all within your *conscious* control when you awaken to the incredible world of lucid dreaming.

What is a Lucid Dream?

When we normally dream, it is usually not until *after* we wake up in the morning that we realize we have been dreaming. When we talk about a *lucid* dream, we are aware that we are dreaming *while* we are dreaming and suddenly the dream scenery becomes very vivid and realistic – as *real* as *waking* life – and then some! The colors are brighter, *more* life-like, almost lumunescent in quality as they shimmer and pulsate with beauty. In a lucid dream, you *know* you are dreaming *while* you are dreaming. You *know* you are in a bed asleep while this experience is going on. You *know* that that all of these incredibly "real" looking images are part of a "dream." In a lucid dream, you can eat a chocolate cake and have a *real* sensation of taste *and* smell of chocolate in your "mouth" and "nose." These sensations are just as real and indistinguishable as you could ever possibly experience in waking life!

Once lucid, you can walk naked along the white sands of Bermuda with a beautiful island native and actually *feel* real sand under your feet and feel the sun-warmed body of your companion rubbing sensuously next to yours. A lucid dream is as "real" as any real waking life experience with every one of your five senses in full play, including your "sixth sense" or your psychic sense to perceive events that have yet to happen. The only distinguishable difference between a waking experience and a *lucid* dream is that in a lucid dream you *know* you are dreaming; during the day, we just don't know we are in the daytime dream we call "reality." (If you think that waking world reality has any more permanence than dream world reality, then seriously ask yourself, "How long does the *present* moment last?")

The key characteristic of lucid dreams which makes them different form ordinary dreaming is that the moment you *realize* you are dreaming, the nature and visual texture of the dream *immediately* changes and mimics waking world reality to the "Nth" degree.

Aside from the amazing vivid imagery you experience when you become lucid, you can also *create* almost any *world* or adventure you desire. You can learn how to take control and guide your dreams in directions you wish them to go! Wow!

"Feeling is believing."–
Anonymous

The Twilight Zone Episode "Shadow Play"

I first saw this original black and white TV episode of the Twilight Zone back on May 5, 1961, starring Dennis Weaver and written by the brilliant Charles Beaumont. Although I didn't know it at the time, this was an episode of a man who was having a very bad and recurrent *lucid dream*–every night–where he was sentenced to death to be executed. He *knew* that he was dreaming and he often *argued with his dream characters* that they were only figments of his imagination. A stay of execution arrives too late, and he is sentenced to death. He wakes up screaming, knowing that later that night he would repeat the same panic of the dream again knowing that he is dreaming, knowing what will happen, with just a slight change of the roles of the same characters, yet feeling all the terror and anguish nonetheless.

How to Induce Lucid Dreams at Will

"Oh Lord, thou givest us everything at the price of effort."–Leonardo da Vinci

Lucid dream induction (or programming) is a nightly procedure that for many will become a new way of life. These nocturnal procedures should be allotted at least a 21-day trial period before deciding that they won't work for you. You should faithfully perform the following set of instructions without missing a day. Should you miss a day of practice, *you should start again* the following day and from that point begin again another 21-day period as day one. If you are like the majority of the people who have loyally tested this lucid dream induction method, *you will have one* or *several* lucid dreams during this period. If for some reason you do not have a lucid dream during this period, it's more likely than not that certain morning waking habits, such as immediately jumping out of bed to the sound of an alarm clock, or hurriedly rushing to work are counterproductive to your *remembering* your dreams, lucid or otherwise. My advice is to always give it another 21-day period, and usually during the first week or so of the *second* 21-day period, you *will* have full-blown, lucid dreams.

Once lucid dreams begin to happen, there is a tendency, providing that you keep up with your nocturnal procedures, for them to *continue* to happen more and more until you are literally having them each night at will!

Over my more than thirty years of research and study into the phenomena of conscious dream control, I've studied and mastered some very exciting techniques for inducing lucid dreams. The effectiveness of these techniques will always be in direction proportion to your motivation, desire and willingness to follow through faithfully with what has to be done. Once you have your first lucid dream and realize the awesome breathtaking potential of the experience, you will be hooked to practicing faithfully the procedures which follow. Having the mental capability of lucid dreaming will put you in the top 5% of people.

The Visualization-Affirmation Method of Lucid Dream Induction

One of the easiest and most reliable methods for inducing regular lucid dreams is the *Visualization–Affirmation Method*. There are two phases to this method which are:

I. The Pre-Bed Phase

II. The Middle-of-the-Night Phase

The Pre-Bed Phase

The Pre-Bed Phase is the preparatory phase. One of the first prerequisites to the success of lucid dream induction is to go to bed early enough to get a long and restful night of sleep. Avoid going to bed when you begin to get sleepy that you become tired. Doing pre-bed visualization and affirmation when you have gotten too sleepy and tired will be counterproductive to achieving the results that you desire. The key is to prepare for bed an hour *before* the usual time you get sleepy. If you usually *begin* to feel sleepy at 10:00 p.m., then start your pre-bed visualization/affirmation exercise at 9:00 p.m. and go to bed *no later than* 9:50 p.m. This will assure a night of restful, refreshing sleep, which is absolutely necessary for the successful induction of lucid dreams.

"Sleep...peace of the soul, who puttest care to flight."– Ovid

Find a straight-backed chair preferably without arms, and sit with your spine erect, feet flat on the floor and your hands placed comfortably in your lap, palms facing upward, gently close your eyes, and take a *slow* and deep breath in through your nose. As you do this, imagine a small ball of white light about the size of a baseball in the area of your solar plexus located about three inches below the area where your rib cage meets at a "V" and about three inches above the navel. (The solar plexus is an important network of nerves in the middle of the abdomen.) Exhale *slowly* through the mouth, and as you do, see the white ball of light getting bigger. Inhale slowly a second time, and continue to see the ball of white light growing larger inside of you; imagine this white light to be *a source of lucid dream energy* that you will take to bed with you. Exhale slowly through your mouth; the white light begins to encompass your entire body in a bright bubble of shimmering energy. Inhale slowly for a third time as this bright bubble of light now surrounds your body *five feet in all directions*. Exhale and imagine the light become so bright that it lights up the entire room. Upon completing each of your three slow deep breaths, using the white light energy, direct now all of your attention to your brow area at the point located in the middle of the forehead. Imagine as though you are looking out through this area as though it were a peephole or window. Keep your attention fixed on this area throught the *entire* exercise.

Looking out through the middle of your forehead, see a white movie projection screen about five feet in front of you. Onto this mental screen, you will project the desired images and affirmations. See this mental screen take up your entire visual field. See, word by word, in bright golden letters of pure light the following affirmation, "I will wake up at the best time tonight to induce a lucid dream." See each word appear one-by-one in succession and then gently fade to be followed by the next word, then the next in very bright golden light. Repeat this "visual" affirmation for a total of five times. *Feel* the meaning of the words you are mentally seeing and repeating. Feel the excitement and anticipation in your solar plexus (also known as your "gut"); this is *very* important.

When you have completed your fifth visual affirmation, you now begin the creative visualization. On your same mental screen, see yourself lying in bed and you imagine yourself suddenly waking after a dream. You think, "It is now time to program a lucid dream." You first see yourself jotting down the dream from which you just woke. (Keep in my that all of this is a visualization of what you will be doing.) Then see yourself get up to go to the bathroom if you need to, and then go back into your bedroom. You then see yourself sitting down in your favorite meditation chair that you would normally place next to your bed. You imagine yourself *beginning* your lucid dream induction procedures of Phase II (The-Middle-of-the-Night Phase) as will be described thoroughly in the section which follows. The *Pre*-Bed Phase should take about fifteen minutes.

"Whate'er we leave to God, God does and blesses us."–
Henry David Thoreau

The Middle-of-the-Night Phase

The Middle-of-the-Night Phase is the phase where you actually tell yourself that you will have a lucid dream and what you will have a lucid dream about. At this point, you may ask, "Why should I program to wake up in the middle of the night? Why not just program a lucid dream before I go to bed and eliminate the need to have to get up in the middle of the night?" To simply program yourself with the phrase, "When I dream tonight, I will realize I am dreaming" is indeed possible and *will* work, but on a much more limited scale that this super-effective Two-Phase Visualization/Affirmation Method. By only programming, "When I dream tonight, I will realize I am dreaming" several times and then going to bed for the rest of the night will give you about one lucid dream per week (which is great!), but the Two-Phase Method will eventually allow you to experience lucid dreams every night at will. There is another very important reason for adoption of this two-phase lucid dream induction method and that is all experienced lucid dreamers have noted that at least three or four hours of sleep are needed before lucid dreams become easy to produce.

Overcoming Your Initial and Natural Resistance to Get Up

In spite of all of the effectiveness of this two-phase method, there is a serious drawback. You will have to overcome your very natural and initial resistance to get up from the comfort of your bed covers and the warmth of your partner (if you have one) to do your programming. Take heart, though the resistance is initial, if you make yourself do it for at least one week, it will become easier and easier. In practically no time, it will be natural and automatic. This is why you must always retire to bed *before* you get too sleepy. You should go to bed early enough to allow for a *restful* night of sleep. This allows you to get up with much less difficulty in the middle of the night during your pre-dawn period. One other thing, don't stay up too longer doing other things that tend to wake you up too completely; a little drowsiness is good. If you stay up too long reading or doing other things, you may rouse yourself a little too much and then find some difficulty later on falling back to sleep. Try to begin your visualization/affirmation lucid dream induction meditation within five minutes after having gotten up. Even if you do experience a little insomnia or difficulty in falling back to sleep during the first few nights of practice, it tends to disappear within a few days of practice. Before you know it, you will be falling asleep within seconds of touching your head onto the pillow.

"Do what you can, with what you have, where you are." – Theodore Roosevelt

The Step-by-Step Procedure Phase II for Lucid Dream Induction

a) You wake up spontaneously after a dream in the middle of the night (as programmed).

b) Without moving, recall this last dream, and begin to record it on your bedside note pad with your eyes closed (as previously instructed).

c) Make a special note of any strange scenes or images.

d) Get up and go to the restroom if you need to.

e) Return back to your bedroom, and sit in your meditation chair.

f) Take three, very slow, deep breaths. Breathe in for the count of ten and exhaling for a count of ten. Repeat this cycle two more times for a total of three. From the first breath cycle, mentally extend the white light starting at the solar plexus, gradually encompassing the entire body in an egg-shaped sphere of luminous lucid dream energy by the end of the third breath cycle.

g) Direct your attention to the middle of the forehead between the eyes in the area of the brow. Mentally look out through this area, as though it were an opening or window revealing a pure white movie screen about five feet in front of you, taking up your entire visual field. Onto this screen, see your desired affirmation appear in bright, golden light flashing on, word by word, in front of you. Sample affirmations could be:

1) "Next time I'm dreaming, I will dream of meeting my future soul mate, and I will realize I am dreaming!"

2) "Next time I'm dreaming, I will dream of conversing with Albert Einstein, and I will realize I am dreaming!"

3) "Next time I'm dreaming, I will dream of visiting realms of heaven, and I will realize I am dreaming!"

h) Repeat your selected affirmation for at least three times in the same manner.

i) Following your affirmations, you now begin a special creative visualization:

Recall the dream from which you just woke (or recall *any* dream you have had recently) and see it through the middle of your forehead onto the white mental screen that is five feet in front of you. Carefully replay the dream from beginning to end. Try to recall the most unusual image of the dream. Upon reviewing this strange image, imagine that you suddenly realize that you are dreaming within this dream. Upon imagining yourself becoming conscious that you are dreaming, see the dream landscape become vivid and realistic. See yourself doing and saying all the things that you would like to do and say in this dream. Picture yourself then waking up the next morning, calling a friend and sharing with him your lucid dream success.

j) Repeat this entire affirmation/creaative visualization procedure two more times, then get up, and go back to sleep.

If you do this procedure each night, you *will* have lucid dreams!

"If you don't stand for something, you'll fall for anything."–Michael Evans

Give it however, the necessary twenty-one day minimum trial period. The Affirmation/Visualization Lucid Dream Induction Procedure is an amazingly simple and effective technique.

How to Control a Lucid Dream

Unlike waking reality, there is a certain instability about lucid dreams images. They tend to change and morph quite easily until you develop some techniques for controlling them. There are some very well-known phases of lucid dreaming that the experienced lucid dreamer goes through.

The *Pre-Lucid* Phase of Lucid Dream Control

The Pre-Lucid Phase is when your critical faculty begins to exercise itself within the dream. You begin to question (within the dream) whether or not a certain strange image or event is real or is in fact a dream. When this begins to happen, you would do what's called a "reality test." By this I mean you would do something that you normally would not be able to do in the three-dimensional waking world. Jump up in the air, and if you last in midair for even a few seconds, you would *know* you must be dreaming; you will thus become lucid. Now there is a small problem for novices of the lucid dream experience, and that is that the sudden vividness of the life-like images may be too surprisingly exciting for you (like the first time you had an orgasm) and you may simply wake yourself up and thus cut short your lucid dream experience. The key to lucid dream control is to maintain a state of "detached interest." You don't want to get *too* excited.

Stabilizing Your Lucid Dream Experience

If your lucid dream images begin to waiver and vacillate, you may stabilize them by simply looking briefly at your "dream hands" until this image becomes clear. You then look again at any object in the room or place where you find yourself in the dream landscape. Notice now that the object stabilizes itself and comes into sharp, clear focus. Repeat this process of looking back and forth from the palms of your hands to other objects in the room, until you have completely brought them all into clear focus. Enjoy all the sense experience of your vivid, lucid dream: the sights, the tastes, the smells, etc.

False Awakenings

When a dream is about to end, you will most likely experience another phenomenon of the lucid dream called, the False Awakening. A false awakening happens when a lucid dream finishes and you *dream* that you are waking. Within seconds of dreaming that you are waking, you will then follow with the *real* awakening to your daytime world of three-

"O bed! O bed! Delicious bed! That heaven on earth to the weary head."–Thomas Hood

dimensional reality.

In the beginning, you may have only one or two lucid dreams per week, but with each lucid dream experience, you will find that your ability to have them automatically increases more and more, until you are having at least one incredible and fantastic dream each and every night.

The Awesome Possibilities of Lucid Dreams

Just to contemplate the creative possibilities of the lucid dream state is breathtaking. At night, those without sight could see. Those without speech could talk. The elderly could experience youth. A shy person could practice confidence. An could create new paintings. An architect could see new cities. Scientific exploration. Creative problem-solving. Health and inner growth. Sensual recreation. All this and more is possible and awaits *you* as you sleep and dream tonight!

"Health is the first muse, and sleep is the condition to produce it." –Ralph Waldo Emerson

"You are not only who you are today but also who you choose to become tomorrow."–
Melvin Powers

CHAPTER 17

Final Thoughts: Who Are You?

This is going to be by far the shortest chapter in the book, yet paradoxically it maybe one of the most important. Before we go, let me ask you a question, and I want you to take a moment before you answer it to yourself. Who *are* you? Let us assume for a moment that you are not your body. Let us assume likewise that you are not the thoughts that come and go in and out of your mind. How can something so impermanent as thought be the permanence of who you are? *If*, and this is a big if, you are not your body or your mind, or your thoughts, then in essence, who *are* you?

The Divine Syllogism

"With God, all things are possible." "All things are possible to him who believes." <u>Then</u> he who believes–becomes–*God in action!*

Peace. Love. Infinite joy–and fulfillment–be always with you.

"When I look at the future, it's so bright, it burns my eyes." –Oprah Winfrey

Required Book Reading

The Power of Now, Eckhart Tolle. ISBN 1-57731-480-8 $14.00

The Magic, Rhonda Byrne. ISBN 978-1-4516-7344-9 $12.99

The Automatic Millionaire, David Bach. ISBN 0-7679-1410-4 $19.95

The Secret, Rhonda Byrne. ISBN 1-58270-170-9 $23.95

The Silva Mind Control Method, José Silva. ISBN 0-6717-3989-1 $7.99

Ultimate Secret to Getting Absolutely Everything You Want, Mike Hernacki. ISBN 0-425-17827-7 $11.95

Think and Grow Rich, Napoleon Hill. ISBN 0-87980-444-0 $12.00 (www.mpowers.com)

You'll See It When You Believe It, Wayne Dyer. ISBN 0-0994-7429-8 $14.45

Required Car Audiobooks on CD

Lucid Dreaming, Stephen LaBerge. ISBN 1-59179-150-2 $19.95

Rich Dad, Poor Dad, Robert T. Kyosaki. ISBN 1-5862-1091-2 $24.98

Secrets of the Millionaire Mind, T. Harv Eker. ISBN 0-0607-7657-9 $22.95

The Automatic Millionaire, David Bach. ISBN 0-7435-3841-2 $29.95

The Secret on CD's, Rhonda Byrne. ISBN 1-7435-6619-X $29.95

The Secret on DVD, Rhonda Byrne. <u>Highly</u> Recommended! (Not for car listening) $29.99

Think and Grow Rich: The 21st Century Edition, Napoleon Hill. ISBN 0-9324-2928-X $49.95

Turn Your Debt Into Wealth, John M. Cummuta. ISBN 0-7435-2519-1 $30.00

You'll See It When You Believe It, Wayne Dyer. ISBN 0-7435-2911-1 $19.95

 **CHARLES PROSPER, M.A.,** entrepreneur, educator, personal growth specialist and author of more than 10 books, has practiced The 12 Great Laws all of his professional career. He is dynamic, charismatic and knowledgeable who walks the walk in everything that he teaches in his workshops and seminars. Mr. Prosper holds a Masters Degree in Psychology from North Central University of Prescott, Arizona.

Quick & Easy Order Form

Yes, please rush me the following:

❏ The 12 Laws of Success (the Book)..$20.00
❏ How to Use the 12 Great Laws of Success: 3-Hour Live Seminar (DVD)..............................$77.00

Shipping by Air U.S. : $5.00 for one book and $2.00 each additional item (same order). _____

Sales Tax: Please add 10 % for products shipped to California addresses. _____

TOTAL OF ORDER _____

Please email me more FREE information on:

❏ Teleseminars   ❏ Audiobooks   ❏ DVD's   ❏ Seminars   ❏ **Success Focus Groups**

❏ Please charge my credit card: ❏ Mastercard ❏ Visa

_____   _____
Credit Card #   Exp. Date

_____   _____
Name as it appears on card   Signature

_____   ❏ Check   ❏ Money Order
The last three security digits on back of credit card

Name _____

Address _____

City _____ State _____ Zip _____

Daytime Phone # _____
                            (in case we have a question on your order)
Email _____

Email, call, or mail to: Charles Prosper (Global Publishing Company)
                            2658 Griffth Park Blvd. Suite 349
                            Los Angeles, CA 90039
                            (323) 351-4516 *phone*
                            prosperme7@hotmail.com
                            **(Email me your requests for FREE information -
                            especially the Prosper Success Focus Groups.)**

(To keep from tearing your book, you may photocopy the order form. Thank you.)

Quick & Easy Order Form

Yes, please rush me the following:

❑ The 12 Laws of Success (the Book)..$20.00
❑ How to Use the 12 Great Laws of Success: 3-Hour Live Seminar (DVD)..............................$77.00

Shipping by Air U.S.: $5.00 for one book and $2.00 each additional item (same order). _____

Sales Tax: Please add 10 % for products shipped to California addresses. _____

TOTAL OF ORDER _____

Please email me more FREE information on:

❑ Teleseminars ❑ Audiobooks ❑ DVD's ❑ Seminars ❑ **Success Focus Groups**

❑ Please charge my credit card: ❑ Mastercard ❑ Visa

_____   _____
Credit Card #   Exp. Date

_____   _____
Name as it appears on card   Signature

_____   ❑ Check   ❑ Money Order
The last three security digits on back of credit card

Name _____

Address _____

City _____ State _____ Zip _____

Daytime Phone # _____

(in case we have a question on your order)

Email _____

Email, call, or mail to: Charles Prosper (Global Publishing Company)
2658 Griffth Park Blvd. Suite 349
Los Angeles, CA 90039
(323) 351-4516 *phone*
prosperme7@hotmail.com
(Email me your requests for FREE information - especially the Prosper Success Focus Groups.)

(To keep from tearing your book, you may photocopy the order form. Thank you.)

Quick & Easy Order Form

Yes, please rush me the following:

❑ The 12 Laws of Success (the Book)..$30.00
❑ How to Use the 12 Great Laws of Success: 3-Hour Live Seminar (DVD).............................$77.00

Shipping by Air U.S.: $5.00 for one book and $2.00 each additional item (same order). _____

Sales Tax: Please add 10 % for products shipped to California addresses. _____

TOTAL OF ORDER _____

Please email me more FREE information on:

❑ Teleseminars   ❑ Audiobooks   ❑ DVD's   ❑ Seminars   ❑ **Success Focus Groups**

❑ Please charge my credit card: ❑ Mastercard ❑ Visa

_____   _____
Credit Card #   Exp. Date

_____   _____
Name as it appears on card   Signature

_____   ❑ Check   ❑ Money Order
The last three security digits on back of credit card

Name _____

Address _____

City _____ State _____ Zip _____

Daytime Phone # _____
                    (in case we have a question on your order)

Email _____

Email, call, or mail to: Charles Prosper (Global Publishing Company)
                           2658 Griffth Park Blvd. Suite 349
                           Los Angeles, CA 90039
                           (323) 351-4516 *phone*
                           prosperme7@hotmail.com
                           **(Email me your requests for FREE information -
                           especially the Prosper Success Focus Groups.)**

(To keep from tearing your book, you may photocopy the order form. Thank you.)